Rivers in World History

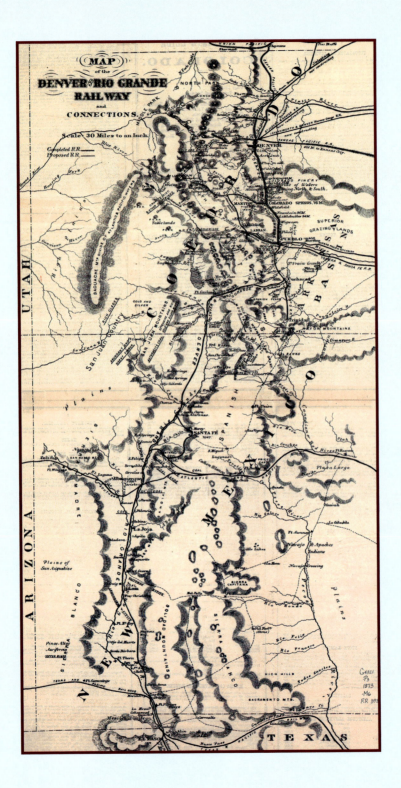

THE RIO GRANDE

Tim McNeese

CHELSEA HOUSE
PUBLISHERS

A Haights Cross Communications Company

Philadelphia

FRONTIS: The Denver & Rio Grande Railway parallels the Rio Grande in the center of this 1873 map. The source of the Rio Grande, North America's fifth-longest river, lies in Colorado's San Juan Mountains (left-center part of the map) and it flows nearly 1,900 miles until it reaches the Gulf of Mexico.

CHELSEA HOUSE PUBLISHERS

VP, NEW PRODUCT DEVELOPMENT Sally Cheney
DIRECTOR OF PRODUCTION Kim Shinners
CREATIVE MANAGER Takeshi Takahashi
MANUFACTURING MANAGER Diann Grasse

Staff for THE RIO GRANDE

EXECUTIVE EDITOR Lee Marcott
EDITOR Christian Green
PRODUCTION EDITOR Noelle Nardone
PHOTO EDITOR Sarah Bloom
SERIES AND COVER DESIGNER Keith Trego
LAYOUT 21st Century Publishing and Communications, Inc.

A Haights Cross Communications Company

First Printing

9 8 7 6 5 4 3 2 1

Library of Congress Cataloging-in-Publication Data

McNeese, Tim.
    The Rio Grande/written by Tim McNeese.
        p. cm.—(Rivers in world history)
Includes bibliographical references and index.
Audience: Grades 9-12.
    ISBN 0-7910-8244-X
    1. Rio Grande—History—Juvenile literature. I. Title. II. Series.
F392.R5M39 2005
976.4'4—dc22

                                                        2004018760

All links and Web addresses were checked and verified to be correct at the time of publication. Because of the dynamic nature of the Web, some addresses and links may have changed since publication and may no longer be valid.

CONTENTS

1

Ancient River; Ancient People

The Rio Grande flows down from the mountains of the southern Rockies, cutting its twisted course across this region of the American Southwest like a desert snake. With a length of nearly 1,900 miles, the Rio Grande ranks as the fifth longest river on the North American continent; it is the second longest American river after the Missouri-Mississippi system. Only 19 other rivers around the world are longer. Although hundreds of miles of the Upper Rio Grande cut across New Mexico, much of the southern portion of the river—approximately two-thirds of the river's total length—serves as an international border between the state of Texas and the northern Mexican states of Chihuahua, Coahuila, Nuevo León, and Tamaulipas. Mexicans, in fact, call the river Río Bravo del Norte (the wild river of the north).

The Rio Grande descends toward the Gulf of Mexico by slicing its way across desert lands and steppes. On its way toward the Gulf, the Rio Grande provides much-needed irrigation for the extensive farming lands that lie beyond its banks. More than two million acres of agricultural lands are watered by the Rio Grande, with just over half of those acres lying in Mexico. Thanks to irrigation, arid lands that would produce little without the Rio Grande's waters produce great harvests of potatoes and grasses, such as alfalfa, in Colorado, as well as a variety of vegetable crops, citrus fruits, and cotton in the river's lower reaches. Although modern farming relies heavily on irrigated water from the Rio Grande, the practice is not new to the region. Native Americans were irrigating their farmlands with water from the Rio Grande hundreds of years ago.

The regional watershed of the Rio Grande covers a large portion of the Southwest, a total of nearly 340,000 square miles. Given the region's arid climate, only a little more than half of that area—176,000 square miles—provides tributary river flows that feed the Rio Grande. Three sources supply the initial waters of the Rio Grande, each located in the high country of southern Colorado, more than two miles above sea level. The Rio Grande proper is joined by Spring Creek and South Fork, which flow from the mountains, down to the east. Downstream, several rivers provide tributary waters that feed the Rio Grande, including Rock Creek, Alamosa Creek, Trinchera Creek, and the Conejos River, all flanking the San Luis Valley in Colorado. In New Mexico, the Puerco, Red, and Chama Rivers add their cold mountain waters to the Rio Grande's flow. Other sources include four great draws—Galisteo Creek, the Jemez River, Rio Puerco, and Rio Salado—that are generally dry except when great rain storms deliver great pours of water into their dusty beds.

As the Rio Grande moves south and becomes the border of Texas and Mexico, the Pecos and Devils Rivers become part of the confluence. From the Mexican side, the Río Conchos and the Río San Juan are tributaries. The Río Conchos is a vital addition to the flow of the Rio Grande. As the great river crosses desert lands, it would peter out if not for this additional water supply. A second Salado River, this one flowing out of the Coahuila Mountains of northern Mexico, also reaches the Rio Grande. All these tributaries contribute to the flow of the Rio Grande's nearly 2,000-mile course. The Rio Grande proper rarely carries a large volume of water. Along some of its length, it barely flows at all. There are even places and times when its bed is dry. In many of the locales in which the Rio Grande flows, the annual rainfall averages a paltry five inches.

The source waters of the Rio Grande trickle out of the San Juan Mountains of the Colorado Rockies from an elevation of 12,000 feet above sea level. This stream cuts a narrow path across southern Colorado for a short distance before it reaches the landscape of northern New Mexico. For much of the river's length, as much as three-fourths of its course, it remains within sight of mountains. As the river flows across the San Luis Valley of southern Colorado, one of the largest mountain valleys in the world, its banks are flanked by spruce, fir, and aspen trees. Beyond the San Luis Valley, the Rio Grande flows into the Rio Grande Gorge and northern New Mexico's White Rock Canyon. The Rio Grande Gorge runs for 50 miles, and its canyon walls rise nearly vertically, more than 800 feet above the river. Past these canyonlands, the river flows across the broad plains region of the Basin and Range, as well as the Mexican Plateau. As the river approaches the Big Bend region of western Texas, its waters cut through three additional canyons and nestles its way between gorge walls extending to heights of 1,500 feet and more. Along the final length of the river, the coastal plain causes the Rio Grande to spread out. The great river slows down as its waters meander sluggishly across a coastal delta near the Gulf of Mexico. (For additional information on this area of West Texas, enter "Big Bend" into any search engine and browse the many sites listed.)

The Rio Grande changes dramatically as it makes its way from the mountain heights of the southern Rockies to the Gulf Coast, passing through several temperature zones. In Colorado's mountains, snowfall is common, and ice sheathes the river during most months of the year. As the river cuts through the northern New Mexican mesa lands, the climate is more temperate. When the river reaches the Texas-Mexico desert lands, the climate becomes warmer. Near the Gulf Coast, the Rio Grande passes through an arid climate, where temperatures often hover around 100°F.

These various climate zones impact the river's temperature. At its source, the Rio Grande's waters in January average an icy 14 degrees. Even in mid-summer, its headwaters average 50 degrees. Here the river is new, crystalline, and clear, "in the colors of obsidian, with rippling folds of current like the markings on a trout."[1] As it passes through fertile valleys, red-rock canyons, and desert shelves, it takes on a heavy silt

The Big Bend area of the Rio Grande lies in West Texas, where it cuts a 118-mile northward path between the Chisos Mountains in Texas and the Sierra Madre Oriental in Mexico. The river forms the southern border of the Big Bend National Park and serves as the boundary between the United States and Mexico in this area.

content that darkens its waters to an earthen brown. The silt slows the Rio Grande's flow to a crawl.

CREATING THE GREAT RIVER

Flowing through an environment marked by ancient mountains and exotic valleys, the Rio Grande has etched its course through many years of geologic history. The river did "not actually carve out the depression it follows, except in a minor way."[2] Instead, the primary influence on the river was the underlying geologic features that created a long rift valley that slices New Mexico geographically into two halves from north to south.

Ancient geologic activity involving the formation of the Rocky Mountain chain provides the answer for how the Rio Grande was formed. According to geologists, the western North American continent experienced a geologic upheaval approximately 20 million years ago when the North American geologic plate shifted and collided along the eastern parallel of its neighboring geologic form, the Pacific plate, which runs along the Pacific Coast of California. The resulting geologic movement and pressure caused an "upwarp" that resulted in the formation of the Rocky Mountains as well as several other lesser mountain ranges, including California's Sierra Nevada. The geologic shift was so extreme that the landscape of the southern Rockies rose 5,000 feet.

Within the same geologic time frame, another important event occurred in the same region. The earth's surface "stretched and brittle crust formed a series of rifts, sometimes . . . called troughs or valleys."[3] Nearly all these newly formed rifts were created separately from one another and resulted in the formation of several lakebeds from northern Colorado to southern New Mexico. Over geologic time, these separated rifts began to fill with significant levels of lava and volcanic ash as well as wind-, water-, and erosion-driven soil and rock. After millions of years, the rifts joined together to form an extensive single-trough system. Geologists call this system, which runs through Colorado, New Mexico, and the Mexican state of Chihuahua, the Rio Grande rift. As these initially distinct topographical valleys combined, the lakes (perhaps dozens of them) joined together and formed the flow region of the Rio Grande. With continuing water flow provided by annual snowmelt, the course of the Rio Grande was naturally extended until its channel ultimately reached south to the Gulf of Mexico.

Today, the entire course of the Rio Grande is divided into three parts: the Upper, Middle, and Lower Rio Grande. The Upper Rio Grande flows out of the 12,000-foot heights of the San Juan Mountains of southern Colorado, where the annual snowmelt provides its fresh waters. It flows eastward for 125 miles to Alamosa, located in south-central Colorado. As it reaches the end of its first leg, the river drops in elevation by 4,500 feet.

From Alamosa, the Rio Grande continues arcing to the south, reaching the northern New Mexico border in less than 50 miles. Flowing south through New Mexico, the river passes the cities of Taos and Espanola. Here, the waters of the Rio Grande are joined by the Rio Chama, flowing from the west. Farther south, the river reaches New Mexico's largest city, Albuquerque, where it slows down, having dropped approximately 8,000 feet from its headwaters. Cutting its course along a nearly level plain, the river reaches its center portion, the Middle Rio Grande. To this point, the Rio Grande has flowed 325 miles.

The Middle Rio Grande is the shortest of the three riverine segments. Covering only 130 miles from Albuquerque to the oddly named town of Truth or Consequences, New Mexico, the Rio Grande slips across an arid landscape, a portion of the Chihuahua Desert. In this region, where the annual rainfall is rarely higher than six inches, the river receives little additional water. Here, there are only a handful of tributaries and several of these do not have a continuous annual flow; they dry up as dusty washes through much of a typical year. The arid environment of the region also causes significant evaporation, equal to billions of gallons of water. The result is a drastic decline in the river's flow between Albuquerque and Truth or Consequences.

Before the Rio Grande reaches Truth or Consequences, however, Elephant Butte Dam, the river's largest impounding facility, helps to contain a portion of the river's flow in a vast reservoir. The river continues its southward flow another

200 miles past Elephant Butte until it reaches El Paso, Texas. Here, the river alters its general direction, first turning north for 100 miles and then southeast for the next 325 miles. The 100-mile northward stretch is called Big Bend. Along this part of the river, the Rio Grande passes through scenic canyonlands, which make up part of Big Bend National Park. Beyond Big Bend, the river receives new water from the Mexican Conchos River and the Pecos. As the Rio Grande approaches the Gulf Coast, it moves into a delta region, flowing at a low elevation of approximately 30 feet above sea level. This is an extensive delta that spreads out across the southwestern landscape and covers 5,000 square miles, an area almost equally divided between Texas and Mexico.

THE ARRIVAL OF THE FIRST HUMAN BEINGS

Despite the hostile climate and geography through which the Rio Grande passes, human occupation in the river's region dates back tens of thousands of years. The land supported tall grasses, cottonwood, mesquite trees, and various shrubs, which could be used by early inhabitants for shelter, fuel for their fires, and even for food. Although modern scientists and anthropologists cannot determine exactly when the first peoples arrived in the region of the Rio Grande, archaeological excavations suggest that the region was settled about 20,000 years ago. The early occupants of the Rio Grande region of the American Southwest were hunters and gatherers, including those who hunted the great Pleistocene animals—prehistoric horses, bison, camels, and the giants of the age, mammoths and mastodons—with stone-tipped spears. While the men usually served as the hunters, the women and children gathered wild fruits, roots, bark, and other edible plants.

Archaeologists and paleontologists have discovered spear points from each hunting era, and by 9000 B.C., the early inhabitants of the Rio Grande region were using Sandia points and Clovis points, named after sites unearthed in New Mexico. By 7000 B.C., many of the large prehistoric animals began to die out, forcing the prehistoric peoples of the Rio Grande to alter their cultures. A renewed emphasis was placed on gathering and collecting wild plants for food. Such natural produce as piñon nuts, the fruit of the yucca plant, various berries, and mesquite beans were an important part of the ancient Native American diet in the Rio Grande region. Farming also became an important source for obtaining food, as early inhabitants began gathering seeds, which they planted in the ground and cultivated.

Although the great animals were disappearing, hunting continued. The hunters turned to smaller game, such as deer, rabbits, lizards, snakes, rodents, desert birds, and even insects for food. Archaeologists in the Rio Grande region have discovered evidence of small-animal hunting along the river's banks. Hunting both large and small animals along such rivers as the Rio Grande increased the odds of success for early hunters; rivers were a water source that attracted prey. Since these early hunters did not yet have access to the horse (the Spanish brought the first horses to the Americas during the 1500s), it was easier to kill an animal along a river, where it was difficult to escape, rather than out on the open desert plains. Along the Rio Grande's banks, archaeologists have unearthed the remains of weapons, including projectile points, as well as large piles of animal bones.

Anthropologists refer to the early hunter-gathers of the region as the Cochise people. They lived in small, scattered encampments, taking shelter in makeshift dome-shaped grass huts called *wickiups*. Many also lived under rock shelters and cliff sides. For hundreds of years, the lifestyles and cultures of these early inhabitants of the Southwest barely changed from one century to the next. Women gathered seeds and nuts, and used millstones to ground them into coarse flour for baking.

THE SPIRIT OF THE RIO GRANDE

The earliest human beings to establish their homes along the banks of the Rio Grande understood how vital the river was to their survival: it provided water for irrigation, farming, and consumption. These ancient peoples also considered the Rio Grande and its tributaries sacred. Thus, the Rio Grande provided for both the physical and spiritual lives of the people of the Southwest.

The Native American concept of the physical world was that all physical things—from the sky to the earth, from rocks to animals—have a spirit. The Rio Grande is no exception. Because the Rio Grande was a great provider of life, the ancient dwellers along the Rio Grande valley raised the river to the status of a deity.

Whereas other rivers in the region dried up during several months of the year, the Rio Grande remained in constant flow, its waters always providing for the people who lived nearby. The river "came from the north beyond knowing, and it went to the south nobody knew where. It was always new and yet always the same. . . . The river was part of the day's prayer."* Some tribes living along the river practiced a "river-feeding ceremony during which tribal fishermen returned captured fish to the river to demonstrate their appreciation for the food the river provided them."**

Sometimes, those living in villages along the river's banks would practice spiritual ceremonies that included the river itself. During one ancient Indian ritual, a special group of holy men went to the river to worship:

Thousands of years passed before maize (or corn) was introduced to the Southwest; the techniques of cultivation reaching the region from Mexico around 2500 B.C. This early corn was smaller than modern varieties; it grew in pods and produced small yields come harvest time. Over the centuries, the crop evolved into larger varieties—some that were drought-resistant —an important development for a regional agriculture that could not depend on regular or even adequate rainfall. In time,

And at that hour the men of the dance came through the sapling groves to the river. The deepening yellow dusk put color on the water. The men came in their ceremonial dress. They took it off and went naked to the river's edge. There they breathed upon the pine bough which they had worn, and the baldrics of rabbit fur, and sometimes the gourd rattles, and cast them upon the sliding surface of the water. They sent their prayers with the cast-off branches and the skins which, wherever they were borne by the river wherever it went, would go as part of that day's pleading will. Then entering the river the men bathed. The brown water played about them and over them and they thanked it and blessed it.***

Over time, stories about the Rio Grande and its spiritual nature became part of the oral tradition of the people who considered the river sacred. According to one legend, two villages faced each other from opposite banks of the Rio Grande. Because the people of the two villages were related, they had their medicine men build a bridge across the river. Once the bridge was completed and in use, however, evil witches turned the span over, causing those crossing to fall into the Rio Grande and turn into fish. The story was told to explain why some Native Americans who lived along the great spirit river of the Southwest did not eat fish; doing so would mean they would be eating "their own bewitched relations."+

* Horgan, vol. 1, 32–33.
** Barter, 42.
*** Horgan, vol. 1, 33.
+ Ibid., 63.

maize became the staple crop of the Southwest. With the relative abundance of food provided by regular corn harvests along the banks and fields of the Rio Grande and its tributaries, the Native American population in the region was able to develop permanent settlements and lifestyles.

During the final stage of the Cochise culture, inhabitants of the region evolved into a new culture group—the San Pedro. These Native Americans cultivated beans and squash, which, along with corn, became the three basics of the regional diet. Known as the Three Sisters, these staple crops provided a common diet to inhabitants of the Southwest. The San Pedro culture also developed a new style of housing, one more permanent than a grass hut. With a greater reliance on farming, these southwestern Natives needed semi-permanent housing, surrounded by garden and farming tracts. By 300 B.C., they were building pit houses, which were often circular in design. They were dug a foot or two into the ground, supported by a framework of log beams, and covered over with brush, grasses, and mud. Each of these simple homes featured a fire pit that was used for cooking and kept occupants warm during chilly winters in the high country of modern-day New Mexico. Within a few more generations, the people of the San Pedro culture were also producing a new art form—clay pottery, a Native American craft that still has an important place among modern Indian cultures in the Southwest.

By 100 B.C., significant cultural changes were again under-way as separate cultures developed in other parts of the Southwest, including the Mogollon culture, which was centered along the southern border between Arizona and New Mexico, and the Hohokam culture in south-central Arizona. Another new culture group—the Anasazi—was also developing. This new culture group originated in the Four Corners region, where the modern-day states of Colorado, Utah, Arizona, and New Mexico meet. It was a culture that developed in stages over several hundred years.

Early Anasazis lived in pit houses, farmed, and engaged in traditional hunting-gathering practices. They also developed new types of snares for trapping animals and new designs for spears, including a device called an *atlatl*—a hand-held catapult that was used to throw short spears farther than traditional spears could be thrown.

The Anasazis, which translates to "ancient ones," or "ancient enemies" in Navajo, are the ancestors of today's Pueblo people and best known for their cliff dwellings (shown here), which the Spanish referred to as pueblos. By the end of the thirteenth century A.D., the Anasazis moved out of these dwellings and settled in the major river valleys of the Southwest, including the Rio Grande.

Later Anasazi culture groups used the bow and arrow, began growing cotton, fashioned turquoise jewelry, created new styles of pottery, and began weaving cotton textiles that were colored with natural vegetable dyes. They also designed elaborate pueblo systems—multistoried homes that were much more complex than anything southwestern Natives of earlier cultures had constructed. Some pueblo buildings were five stories tall. This era of the Anasazi culture lasted more than a 1,000 years.

2

Tribes along
the Rio Grande

By the end of the 1200s, the Anasazis had begun to abandon their pueblo villages and cliff dwellings, and move to other, perhaps more hospitable, sites. Some Anasazis moved to the major river valleys of the Southwest, including the Colorado and the Rio Grande. One major reason for the movement to river valleys and the general abandonment of cliff dwellings and earlier pueblo complexes had to do with the weather. A lengthy drought cycle in the region may have rendered early sites uninhabitable. Over the following centuries, from 1300 until 1550, the Native Americans of the Southwest evolved into their modern tribal identities. The Anasazis became the ancestors of the modern-day Pueblos.

THE "VILLAGE" PEOPLE

The Spanish word *pueblo* means "village," and it was the Spaniards who dubbed the Native Americans they encountered in the Southwest "the Pueblo," a descriptive term that reflected the type of dwelling they inhabited. The name is still used today. The Pueblos were a diverse group, and the word "pueblo" refers to several different Native cultural and tribal divisions. Among these are the Hopis and the Zuñis, who took up residence on the Colorado Plateau. The Hopis lived in what is now Arizona, and the Zuñis lived in the western half of New Mexico, near the Rio Grande. Depending on where in the Southwest the various Pueblo peoples settled, they are identified by modern anthropologists as the "Desert Pueblos" or the "River Pueblos." Those who settled along the banks of the Rio Grande were among the latter. The River Pueblos—sometimes referred to as the Eastern Pueblos—included the following divisions: Santa Ana, San Felipe, Santo Domingo, Cochiti, Zia, Jemez, Sandia, Isleta, Picuris, Taos, Tesuque, Nambe, Pojoaque, San Ildefonso, Santa Clara, and San Juan. These cultural and tribal groups built their scattered villages along the banks of the Rio Grande and its tributaries. At the time of the arrival of the Spanish in the Southwest in

Pueblo del Arroyo, or "Town of the Gully," is located in Chaco Canyon in northwestern New Mexico. Constructed between A.D. 1065 and 1140, Pueblo del Arroyo is composed of several great houses, which are large, multistoried structures with formalized masonry.

the mid-1500s, the total Pueblo population, from the western towns of the Hopis to the settlements of those living in the Rio Grande valley, numbered approximately 16,000. There were about 80 different settlements, each village existing autonomously.

Pueblo villages and towns were generally "compactly built, single, multistoried structures of apartment-like rooms, often constructed, for defensive purposes, on the tops of steep-sided, rocky mesas."[4] These buildings were made of stone or adobe mud or both; they were square or rectangular, sometimes rounded, and rose from various desert or mesa floors in staggered tiers overlooking common plazas and public village gathering places. The larger Pueblo towns covered approximately 10 to 12 acres and featured long streets of connected apartments and other rooms, usually two or three stories in height. Homes faced the town "streets." Many Pueblo dwellings were built with no entrance door on the ground-level floor but featured ladders that the village dwellers used to reach rooftop openings.

As the historical Pueblos diverged into two separate geographical movements—desert or river—they developed different cultures. The River Pueblos developed elaborate irrigation systems, diverting river water across arid fields and turning otherwise dry lands into agricultural oases. They planted a wide variety of crops, including squash, beans, cotton, tobacco, maize, and gourds, and used drilling sticks and hoes to cultivate their lands. The men of these pueblo systems provided the farm labor.

When the first Europeans arrived in the Southwest, they encountered these Pueblo agriculturists and were amazed at their elaborate irrigation systems. One Spaniard, who visited the region in 1583, wrote of "many irrigated corn fields with canals and dams, built as if by the Spaniards."[5] The fields of the Pueblo Indians seen by this visiting Spaniard were extensive: "These people have their fields [six miles] distant from the pueblo, near a medium-sized river, and irrigate their farms by little streams of water diverted from a marsh near the river."[6] The irrigation system of the Pueblos included low-level earthen dams, many no taller than three or four feet, which have been unearthed by modern archaeologists. Multiple "check dams" were built to cause tributary streams to the Rio Grande and other central New Mexican rivers to collect water, increase the amount of water seeping into the ground, and thus irrigate many small patches of planted field crops, including corn, beans, and squash.

Fish were another important food source for Pueblo Indians living along the banks of the Rio Grande and its tributaries. Pueblos did not generally use canoes for fishing; they fished from alongside the riverbanks, sometimes on wooden platforms that extended over the river. Archaeologists have uncovered bone or stone fishhooks, dip nets, seines, fishing spears, and baskets designed to trap unwary fish. Archaeological excavations of special pits at Pueblo dwelling sites, several feet deep, have yielded the skeletal remains of fish as well as caches of fish hooks. Archaeologists believe that "fish may have been stocked in the pits that functioned as fish ponds."[7]

Although the Native Americans along the Rio Grande and its tributaries did not seem to rely on canoes for fishing, they did rely on them for mobility. In a world without the horse, moving about on desert plains and across inhospitable mountains was daunting. Tapping the Rio Grande as a transportation route provided Native Americans with an easier way to get from one village or hunting ground to another. How early the southwestern Indians were using canoes is unclear, but ancient rock art, called petroglyphs, include images of canoes and simple raft designs. Early Native American stories also tell of the use of canoes.

Archaeologists note three types of canoes used by Indians living in the Rio Grande valley: animal skin, bark, and dugout. The animal skin canoe was a small but durable craft that included a wooden frame covered by deer, elk, or moose hides, which served to waterproof the canoe. The bark canoe was often used where trees were plentiful, especially along the Colorado reaches of the Upper Rio Grande. Indians peeled the bark from aspen trees in thin sheets that were sewed tightly together and waterproofed with tree pitch or sap. The dugout canoe was carved from a large, single tree trunk. After felling a tree and allowing it to dry for several months, Native American crafts-men then burned out the central portion, leaving the outer shell of the tree to form the canoe's body. "Burning" a dugout canoe was necessary because adequate axes and other hacking tools were unavailable. These canoes were often quite large, could hold more passengers than either a bark or skin canoe, and lasted longer. They were heavy, however, and less portable than bark or skin canoes when carried overland from one stream to another.

THE APACHES

Another major Indian group also settled along the banks of the Rio Grande. Sometime between 1100 and 1200, a nomadic group of Indians migrated from the north, perhaps as far away as western Canada, and reached the world of the Pueblos in what is now modern-day New Mexico and Texas. Whereas the Pueblos were peaceful, these newcomers were fierce and warlike. The Pueblos called them *apaches*, a word that means "enemies." The Apaches called themselves *Ndee* or *Dine'e*, meaning "the people."

The new people of the Rio Grande region were taller than the average Pueblo, spoke a different language, and soon frag-mented into various regional groups. Some settled in the Four Corners region and became known as the Apache de Nabahu. These were the early Navajo (sometimes spelled Navaho) people. In time, the Navajos developed settlements and social patterns quite different from those of most Apaches. They became farmers and shepherds and were quite peaceful. Other tribes remained warlike, including the Jicarilla Apaches of northern New Mexico, the Mescalero Apaches to the south-west, the Lipan Apaches, who reached the Big Bend of the Rio Grande valley, and the Mimbreno Apaches, who lived

ANCIENT CRAFTS AND MODERN ARTISANS

Native American culture groups of the Southwest began developing the craft of pottery hundreds or even thousands of years ago. Whereas much of this early pottery was designed for strictly utilitarian purposes, modern southwestern pottery making remains an important art form, even if much of the pottery produced is fashioned for its decorative and artistic beauty.

Anthropologists rely on early forms of southwestern pottery to help identify several different ancient cultural groups. The Hohokams, for example, were sometimes known for their "red-on-buff" pottery, which featured tan-colored clay and red-painted patterns and figures. One subculture of the Mogollons, the Mimbre group, developed a style of painted pottery that featured black paint on white clay. Modern-day Native American potters have created their own unique styles as they redefine an ancient art form.

Pueblo men and women still form beautiful pottery pieces, each unique in its own way. The Taos and Picuris Pueblo peoples fashion tan-colored pottery, which remains unpainted but is "decorated" with flecks and glints of reflective mica. The Cochiti and Santo Domingo peoples are known for their cream-colored pottery, which they decorate with black geometric patterns and bird motifs, much in the style of the ancient Mimbres.

One unique and highly prized style of Rio Grande region pottery was created in 1919 at the San Ildefonso pueblo. Potters Maria and Julian Martinez, members of a Tewa-speaking tribe, became famous for their special black-on-black style, having created their first pot of that type purely by accident. While firing some clay pots in a wood fire, Julian allowed the blaze to get too hot, turning their red clay pots completely black. Since the pots were not cracked, as Maria feared they would be, she decided to

west of the Rio Grande. (Others, including the Chiricahua, San Carlos, Tonto, and White Mountain Apaches, spread farther to the west into what is now modern-day Arizona.)

The Apache tribes of the Southwest, including those of the Rio Grande region, lived quite simply. Most lived in grass wickiups, which were circular, conical, or dome-shaped. These basic homes were constructed by women, who erected a framework of cottonwood, willow, or mesquite poles, tied paint them anyway, applying low-sheen black paint to the high-glaze, black pottery. The result was a unique style, one that immediately appealed to the Anglo traders who visited the Martinez' pueblo. The business-shrewd Maria convinced the traders that the black-on-black pots were "special" and charged more than the usual amount.

The Martinezes were already well known for their special pottery-making skills, Maria having practiced the art since childhood. She learned the art from an aunt who was herself a skilled potter. Even while she was in her early 20s, Maria's work was sought by collectors and museums alike. In 1908, the same year she married Julian Martinez, the Museum of New Mexico arranged for her to produce pottery in the same polychromatic style the people of the San Ildefonso pueblo had used hundreds of years earlier. As Maria fashioned the pots, husband Julian painted them. Their work was so highly prized that their pottery was put on display at the 1904 St. Louis World's Fair, the 1915 Panama-California Exposition in San Diego, and the 1934 Chicago World's Fair. Although Julian died prematurely in 1943, Maria lived into her 90s, dying in 1980. Today, Maria's grandson, Tony Da, continues the family practice of pottery making.

Although pottery styles, types, and forms have changed over the centuries, one aspect of Pueblo pottery art has remained the same: Whereas most modern potters use a potter's wheel to form their clay works of art, the Pueblo potters of today still form their pottery by hand—they use the same coiled clay rope technique their ancestors used hundreds or even thousands of years ago.

them together with yucca fiber, and covered them over with brush and bear grass. Many of the wickiups were small but some were quite roomy and provided shelter for several families. Apache clothing was equally simple. The men wore animal skin shirts and breechcloths; the women wore two-piece dresses of the same material. High-topped moccasins were the utilitarian fashion, helping to protect the lower legs from cactus and other menacing plants as well as from snakes.

Apaches of the Rio Grande region lived in wickiups, which were circular, conical, or dome-shaped brush and grass huts supported by a framework of cottonwood, willow, or mesquite poles.

As was typical among many other Natives of the Southwest, Apache women performed the cooking chores and were known for their basket-weaving skills. Historically, some of the best regional basketry was created by Apache women. Among these were coiled baskets of black and brown, featuring geometric shapes and animal and human figures. The men were the hunters, raiders, and horsemen. Apache raids were common, and the primary targets for many Rio Grande Apaches were their neighbors, the Pueblos. Since the Pueblos tended to possess greater wealth in goods and slaves, the Apaches saw them as tempting marks. Most Apache raids were carried out on foot. Ironically, when the Apaches attacked a Pueblo village, they would steal the horses and then eat them, preferring to use them for food rather than to increase mobility. Apache religion mirrored that of other Native American groups. There was a strong reliance on powerful medicine men or women called shamans. Usually older men or women, shamans carried out rituals intended to heal the sick, predict the future, keep illness out of the camps, and guarantee success in everything from raids against an enemy to sexual activity. The Apache pantheon was crowded with a variety of gods. Among them were the *Gans*, mountain spirits who were believed to dwell in the high places of the Rio Grande region. (For additional information on this group of Native Americans, enter "Apache Indian" into any search engine and browse the many sites listed.)

3

The Spanish Arrive

For thousands of years, the various Native American culture groups—the Pueblos, the Apaches, and others—occupied the mountains, valleys, and broad, flat-topped mesas of the Rio Grande region. Although they did not live in complete harmony, they had similar lifestyles. They were all occupants of a vast region, one dominated by the flow of a river of extraordinary length. By the 1300s and 1400s, their various tribal and band identities were fully established, their territorial claims delineated, their sociopolitical practices ingrained, and their religious beliefs an essential part of their lives and their identity.

By the 1500s, however, a new people were arriving in the region of the Rio Grande, people so different that many of the Native Americans who first set eyes on them were not certain they were human beings. The strangers arrived in great boats with giant sails billowing in the warm breezes of the Gulf of Mexico. Their skin was pale, and they wore metal around their chests and on their heads. They spoke a strange language, and they carried wooden and metal sticks that emitted smoke and fire. Perhaps the most curious and startling thing about these newcomers was that they rode a strange and frightening animal, the horse. Both creatures—the strange-looking men and their great four-legged companions—were like nothing the Native Americans of the Rio Grande region had ever seen. The men, of course, were European—the Spaniards.

Following the New World discoveries of the Genoan sea captain and explorer Christopher Columbus during the 1490s, the Spanish government, whose king and queen had sponsored Columbus' explorations, set out to establish extensive colonies in the Caribbean, Mexico, and throughout the region of the Gulf of Mexico and the American Southwest. These lands included the Rio Grande valley. Slowly, but deliberately, the Spanish explored nearly every corner of the Southwest.

Spain's soldier-adventurers, the conquistadors, crisscrossed the lands of Texas, New Mexico, Arizona, and California, as well as the territory of modern-day Mexico.

For much of the sixteenth century, these Spanish explorers repeatedly reached the waters of the Rio Grande, often in search of golden cities and fabled wealth. Although they found little gold during their explorations, they did manage to make contact with many Native American groups. They established trade connections and Catholic missions, all the while mapping lands that were never before seen by Europeans. Although these explorers rarely remained in the Southwest for long, their impact was often permanent. Spain extended its power into those forbidding yet eerily beautiful lands, creating a legacy that continues to the present day.

THE RIVER OF PALMS

In the spring of 1519, four wooden sailing ships, each flying the flag of Spain, set out from Jamaica to explore the coast of the Gulf of Mexico. They were dispatched north, under orders from the Spanish governor of Jamaica, Francisco Garay, to search for a water passage that would lead them across the Americas to the western ocean, the mighty Pacific. Such a route would open the way for Spanish ships to reach the Orient. The captain of the small fleet was Alonso Alvarez de Pineda. Onboard his ships were nearly 300 Spanish soldiers, each eager to stake his claim in the New World in the name of his majesty, the king of Spain. For months, Pineda and his crew searched the coastal lands of modern-day Florida, Louisiana, and Texas, sailing into the mouths of many rivers, inlets, and bays, testing the waters that might lead them to the Far East. By autumn, Pineda's ships had reached the mouth of yet another river whose banks were marked by groves of palm trees. As he had done at other river landings, Pineda laid claim to these new lands:

A small boat was launched over the side to bring Pineda ashore. It was then proper style to step into the surf when the boat grounded and, drawing a sword, slash the blade into the waves, stating at the same time that these waters, and this land, and all in their provinces, now came under the possession of His Most Catholic Majesty.[8]

After months of exploring, Pineda had reached the waters of the Rio Grande. He called his newly discovered stream the Río de las Palmas. Here, Pineda ordered his ships to weigh anchor and remain. After months at sea, his vessels were in desperate need of repair, their "clinker-built planking . . . crusted with barnacles."[9] For 40 days, Pineda's men worked on their vessels, scraping barnacles and recaulking leaky seams. They also made immediate contact with local Indians, trading with them for much-needed food. While their ships were being cleaned and repaired, the Spaniards explored nearly 20 miles up the mouth of the Rio Grande. Along the way, they found 40 Indian villages whose inhabitants lived in homes built of wooden reeds covered with mud. Once the ships were repaired, Pineda and his men set sail for Jamaica. In his reports, the Spanish captain suggested the establishment of a Spanish colony along the Gulf Coast. Of all the rivers and bays he had entered throughout six months of exploration, only one, the mouth of the Rio Grande, was mentioned as a site suitable for colonization.

By the following year, 1520, the governor of Jamaica dispatched a second expedition into the Gulf of Mexico to establish the colony Pineda had proposed the previous year. Three ships under the command of Diego de Camargo reached the Rio Grande that summer. In his company, Camargo had 150 foot soldiers, seven horse-bound conquistadors, several brass cannon, and a handful of masons who were to use the brick and lime onboard the ships to erect a sturdy, permanent fort for the new colony. Only one obstacle stood in the way: Camargo's ships were in poor repair and this would soon prove a problem.

As Pineda had done, Camargo sailed about 20 miles up the Rio de las Palmas and met with local Native Americans. The early encounters were amicable and the trade mutual. In the days that followed, however, fighting broke out. Perhaps the Indians of the Rio Grande realized that the Spaniards intended to build a permanent outpost on their lands. Eighteen of Camargo's men and all seven of the party's horses were killed. Besieged, Camargo and his men managed to reach two of their ships and set sail for open waters. The Natives, however, gave pursuit in a large fleet of canoes. The slow moving Spanish ships and their crew remained constant targets for the Native's arrows and spears until the vessels finally made it to the open water. Without adequate food stores, threatened by hostile Indians, and sailing in ships in bad condition, Camargo and his men abandoned the colony and headed for the Spanish port of Veracruz to the south. Within a matter of weeks, both his ships had sunk, the second while docked in the harbor at Veracruz. A return trip to the Rio Grande would have to be delayed.

On July 25, 1523, after three years had passed, a new contingent of Spanish colonizers arrived at the mouth of the Rio de las Palmas. This time, Governor Garay himself was part of the expedition, accompanied by 750 soldiers onboard 16 ships. The men were heavily armed: their weapons included 200 firearms, 300 crossbows, and several cannon. In spite of their weaponry, they had not come to fight. Oddly enough, they did not even come to stay. Garay was unaware that both earlier efforts to colonize the mouth of the Rio Grande had failed. He had sailed from Jamaica with reinforcements and supplies for the thriving colony he expected to find. Finding no colony, he abandoned his plans. This was the third time the Spanish had failed to establish a colony along the banks of the Rio Grande.

Although Garay continued to dream of building a colony, his dream never materialized. After his death, another Spanish colonial leader, one who had by the mid-1520s established an extraordinary reputation after defeating the Aztec Empire in the interior Valley of Mexico, took up the colonizing plan. His name was Hernando Cortés.

On September 3, 1526, Governor Cortés penned a letter to the king of Spain from Mexico City (the former Aztec capital of Tenochtitlan):

> I have a goodly number of people ready to go to settle at the Rio de las Palmas . . . because I have been informed that it is good land and that there is a port. I do not think God and Your majesty will be served less there than in all the other regions because I have much good news concerning that land.[10]

A combination of intrigues within the Spanish court in Madrid and Cortés reaching beyond his means caused the ambitious Spanish viceroy to lose his grant to build a colony on the Rio Grande. The grant passed into the hands of yet another New World adventurer—Pánfilo de Narváez.

In 1527, armed with a royal charter to erect a colony on the Rio de las Palmas, Narváez left Spain for Cuba. After arriving, he recruited 400 colonists, soldiers for the most part, who, along with 82 horses, boarded five ships and set sail for the Gulf Coast. A strong storm struck the Spanish fleet in April 1528, and Narváez and his men were blown off course. One of his ships crashed onto the breakers off the coast of Florida at Tampa Bay; the others were damaged. Narváez decided to march 300 of his men across the Gulf Coast until they reached the Rio de las Palmas, sending his remaining ships ahead.

After conquering the Aztec Empire in Mexico in the 1520s, Hernando Cortés set his sights on settling the Rio Grande region and searching for the legendary Seven Cities of Cíbola. However, the king of Spain, Charles V, selected Francisco Vásquez de Coronado to lead the expedition and Cortés returned to Spain.

Circumstances did not improve for Narváez. His fleet somehow missed the mouth of the Rio Grande and spent most of a year sailing back and forth from Texas to Florida searching for him. They never found him and finally sailed for Veracruz to the south. As for Narváez and the other members of his land expedition, they struggled along the coast, their numbers depleted by disease, Indian attack, and desertion. After months of difficulty, Narváez and his remaining men—about 250—built crude boats covered with the hides of their horses and attempted to sail south to Mexico. For a month, the boats floated along the coast, never far from land, until they reached the mouth of the Mississippi River. A storm caught the boats and drove them out of sight of one another. Narváez, along with most of his men, was lost in the storm's waves. About 80 men survived; they were washed up on the shores of modern-day Texas, some near Galveston Bay. Among their number was the man appointed by the king of Spain to serve as treasurer of the Rio de las Palmas colony—Álvar Núñez Cabeza de Vaca.

A LEGENDARY SURVIVAL

Cabeza de Vaca was the son of a Spanish nobleman and was accustomed to wealth and power. Shipwrecked on the Texas coast, however, his lineage counted for nothing. Lost in a hostile environment, uncertain of their exact location, Cabeza de Vaca and his comrades held on through a difficult winter. The Narváez expedition had floundered along the East Texas coast near the mouth of the Trinity River in modern-day Galveston. Held captive by the local Indians for several years, Cabeza de Vaca and his comrades worked with and for their captors. The would-be treasurer of a nonexistent colony proved to be a shrewd trader and even practiced rudimentary medicine. (He once removed an arrowhead from a wounded Indian warrior.) As more and more of his comrades died, he became convinced that he must try to return to the safety of Spanish-controlled lands to the south.

Setting out on foot, Cabeza de Vaca struggled across the Texas landscape. He was hungry, his clothing was gone, and he had no firm sense of where he was going. Fortunately, he encountered four men—three ethnic Spaniards and a black Moor who had converted to Christianity—who had also been part of the Narváez expedition and who had survived in another location. The four were living with local Natives. When Cabeza de Vaca stumbled upon them, they were helping the Indians harvest pecans along a small river, one that they referred to as the "river of nuts," probably the Guadalupe River.

For several years, the Spanish survivors trekked across the barren landscape of Texas. Although their exact route is not clearly known today, they probably crossed the south-central portion of Texas. Along the way, they caught their first glimpses of American bison, which Cabeza de Vaca later described in his journal:

> Here also [we] came upon the cows. . . . They appear to me of the size of those in Spain. Their horns are small, like those of Moorish cattle; the hair is very long, like fine wool. . . . Some are brownish and others are black, and to my taste they have better and more meat then those from [Spain]. . . . Of the small hides, the Indians make blankets to cover themselves with, and of the taller ones they make shoes and targets.[11]

By mid-November 1535, Cabeza de Vaca and his companions had reached a group of Indian river villages on the banks of the Rio Grande (near modern-day El Paso). They could not know that they were hundreds of miles from the Gulf Coast on the very same river they had intended to colonize with Captain Narváez—the Rio de las Palmas. The trail these Spanish castaways followed, ironically, did not move south as often as it moved farther west, away from the coastal lands and the relative safety of Spanish towns and outposts in Mexico. One reason was that "on account of natural obstacles they were often deflected northward from their course."[12]

Another reason for the long, circuitous route was that two of Cabeza de Vaca's companions could not swim. This forced the party to search for shallow river fords. In addition, they moved from Indian village to Indian village in a pattern that did not often take them south but west.

Six months after reaching the Rio Grande, Cabeza de Vaca and his men encountered a group of Spanish horsemen who rescued the bedraggled party and took them to a local settlement. At last, Cabeza de Vaca and his companions had returned to Spanish civilization. For eight years, he had suffered hardship and privation in a foreign land. Upon returning to New Spain, he soon told his story of his travels and adventures in the American Southwest, including stories about his journey through the valley of the Rio Grande.

Cabeza de Vaca's adventures inspired other Spanish explorers to follow in his footsteps. Among them was one of history's most famous conquistadors, Francisco Vásquez de Coronado, then governor of Nueva Galicia in western Mexico. By February 1540, Coronado was leading an expedition to the northern lands through which Cabeza de Vaca had passed. There were other stories of these lands that also motivated Coronado, tales told by a priest he had sent into the lands north of his district. Friar Marcos de Niza had wandered through modern-day New Mexico and returned to tell Coronado of a legend about seven cities of gold. These stories of the fabled wealth of Cíbola inspired greed in the Spanish governor, and Coronado set out to find the cities for himself.

The stories proved false. Coronado did manage to reach the Zuñi pueblo of Hawikuh, on the Arizona–New Mexico border, but the Spaniards found little gold. Desperate to discover the fabled cities, Coronado split up his men, sending parties in different directions. Some of his men were the first Europeans to discover the Grand Canyon in modern-day Arizona. Meanwhile, Coronado and his group pushed farther to the east,

ENGLISH SEA DOGS REACH THE UPPER RIO GRANDE

The story of Cabeza de Vaca's shipwreck and adventures in the American Southwest and the valley of the Rio Grande eventually became legendary among his Spanish contemporaries and later generations of Spanish colonists. Cabeza de Vaca's early-sixteenth-century wanderings across the barren lands of the Southwest find their parallel in the later sixteenth-century adventures of three Englishmen who inadvertently found themselves abandoned in a foreign land.

In the fall of 1568, three English sailors—David Ingram, Richard Browne, and Richard Twide—reached the New World aboard a small fleet of ships under the command of the famous English sea dog, Captain Sir John Hawkins. Hawkins' six ships limped into the Mexican coastal town of Veracruz after sailing through a terrible storm; the vessels leaking and in need of repair. Here, the unwelcome English ships were thrown into a battle with Spanish ships, and only two of Hawkins' vessels managed to break out of the Spanish encirclement. One of the beleaguered vessels was captained by Francis Drake, who would later become one of England's most famous sailing commanders and would one day circumnavigate the globe.

Although Drake's ship managed to escape and return to England, the second ship, piloted by Hawkins, slipped up the Gulf Coast, overloaded with survivors from the other lost English vessels. Close to floundering, Hawkins landed 114 of his crewmen on the Gulf beaches 30 miles north of Tampico (at the request of the men themselves). As the ship sailed out of sight to safety, the landed English party began marching north. The march went poorly. Local Indians attacked the English, killing several and scattering the remainder. After a time, Ingram, Browne, and Twide were separated from their companions. Their wanderings eventually led them to the Rio de las Palmas—the Rio Grande. They called it the River of May.

Seeking safety, the three Englishmen made their way along the Rio

reaching the vicinity of present-day Albuquerque and the Rio Grande. It was here that the Spanish explorer and some of his men spent the winter of 1540–1541. The next year, Coronado

Grande. They observed that the lands along the Rio Grande were fertile, noting that "the ground and countrey is most excellent, fertile and pleasant."[*] The wandering Englishmen contrasted the Rio Grande lands with the desert lowlands they had crossed, lands where they observed, "the grasse . . . is not so greene . . . for . . . [it] is burnt away with the heate of the Sunne."[**]

The trio of survivors also observed the local vegetation, investigating the trees and other growth, identifying the various plants, and determining which were edible and which were not. Among their favorites were the local palm trees, quite exotic and fascinating for the Englishmen. The palms became an important source of needed food and drink. By cutting into a tree at a height of two feet from the ground, the explorers tapped a "wine of color like whey, but in taste strong . . . which is most excellent drinke."[***] The inquisitive men also noted that too much of this tree liquid "will distemper both your head and body."[+] They extracted food from the palms, discovering in their tree tops a "most excellent meat raw, after you have pared away the bark."[++] In these palms, the Englishmen also found a medicine, a reddish oil they extracted from the tree's roots, "which is most excellent against poisoned arrowes."[+++] As the men made their way north, they encountered local Indians, dangerous river crossings, and violent storms, including "Turnados" and "Furicanos," similar to the one that had destroyed some of their ships. After a year of carefully following the coast-lands from Mexico to Florida, the intrepid threesome sailed to the northern Atlantic coast and a friendly colony at New Brunswick. By 1569, they were home in England.

[*] Horgan, vol. 1, 152.
[**] Ibid.
[***] Ibid.
[+] Ibid.
[++] Ibid.
[+++] Ibid.

continued east across northern Texas until he finally reached eastern Kansas. Here he found another Native American village, Quivira, the home of the Wichita Indians. (Some modern-day

After being shipwrecked near what is today Galveston, Texas, in 1528, Álvar Núñez Cabeza de Vaca and four of his shipmates were among the first non-Indians to reach Texas. Searching for a way back to Mexico, the group traveled across Texas and survived by becoming traders and healers to the Indians of the region. Finally, after eight years, the party encountered a group of Spaniards on a slave-trading expedition near present-day Sinaloa, on Mexico's Pacific coast, and they were returned to Mexico.

historians place Quivira in the northern panhandle of Texas.) Although Coronado furthered Spain's knowledge of the lands to the north of New Spain, he found no rich cities of gold. Such explorations only convinced the Spanish that the Upper Rio Grande valley had no real value for them. For the remainder of the sixteenth century, Spain generally ignored the region of the Rio Grande from New Mexico to West Texas.

4

Colonizing the Rio Grande

During the 1540s, intrepid Spanish explorer and conquistador Francisco Vásquez de Coronado sought extraordinary riches and cities of gold in the American Southwest. When the Rio Grande valley produced no such wealth for the Spanish crown, the region, considered nothing more than a land of worthless deserts and remote mesas, was almost forgotten. For nearly 40 years after Coronado's expeditions, Spanish officials in New Spain made no effort to explore the lands of the Rio Grande. Similar to earlier explorers, such as Francisco Garay, the Spanish had abandoned their plans to colonize and settle the mouth of the Rio Grande, so Coronado had given up on the pueblo lands bordering the river's northern waters. During much of the remainder of the sixteenth century, the Spanish remained uncertain of the river's actual length; existing maps included only partial legs of the river.

Between 1581 and 1593, however, a new generation of Spanish explorers was inspired to pick up where their predecessors had left off. Several of these second-generation Spanish explorers reached the Rio Grande through a different, more direct route than Coronado had followed. Coronado had swung across the Southwest in a long, sweeping arc that led him across Arizona into northern New Mexico. Later explorers followed the Conchos, the largest of the Rio Grande's tributary rivers, which flowed out of north-central Mexico, its headwaters running from the highlands of the western Sierra Madre.

In 1581, the first of four expeditions marched north along the Conchos. The party included three Catholic priests, Franciscan friars, who were accompanied by nine soldiers and 16 native Mexican servants. The true leader of the party was Fray (Father) Agustín Rodríguez. The friars were intent on converting the Pueblo Indians to the Catholic faith. They reached the juncture of the Conchos and the Rio Grande, a confluence of waters the local Indians called the La Junta de los Rios. The Spanish name for the Rio Grande was the Río de Nuestra

In 1540, Francisco Vásquez de Coronado set out for present-day New Mexico in search of the legendary Seven Cities of Cíbola. Though members of Coronado's party became the first Europeans to see the Grand Canyon, their expedition was deemed a failure because they found no gold, despite traversing most of the Southwest.

Señora de la Concepción. They soon reached the same villages Coronado had visited, including the village complex of Tiguex.

To the east of the Rio Grande, the friars continued to explore, crossing the Pecos River and eventually reaching the western Great Plains. Returning westward, they reached the Acoma pueblo on the Zuñi River, which had also been visited by Coronado, but winter snows drove them back to the Rio Grande. At the pueblo at Puaray, two of the friars announced they would remain to teach the local Natives. Several servants remained with them, but the other members of the expedition returned south.

The next year, a second expedition marched north into the American Southwest. The 19 conquistadors and several Indian servants were led by another priest, Fray Bernardino Beltran.

The soldiers were under the command of a merchant named Antonio de Espejo, who had recently killed one of his ranch workers and was fleeing from Spanish authorities. This second party into the country of the Rio Grande planned to come to the aid of the two priests who had remained in Puaray. On December 9, 1582, the group reached the Rio Grande, naming it Río del Norte. Here they encountered Indians who played musical instruments that gave off an "odd, sweet music, which they played with their mouths, and which sounded like the tones of flutes." [13] Here and there, the party encountered Indians who spoke of other Spanish men, including Cabeza de Vaca. In his reports, Espejo described the Native Americans he and his men encountered in the region of the confluence of the Conchos and Rio Grande:

> We found in some rancherías a number of Indians of the Conchos nation, many of whom, to the number of more than a thousand, came out to meet us along the road we were travel-ing. We found that they lived on rabbits, hares, and deer, which they hunt and which are abundant; and on some crops of maize, gourds, Castilian melons, and watermelons, which they plant and cultivate; and on fish, and the mescales, which . . . they cook . . . and make a preserve like quince jam. It is very sweet and they call it mescale. [14]

Throughout the month of December, the group pushed up the Rio Grande, encountering small crosses that had been placed there by the previous expedition. Farther upriver, the friar and his party finally arrived at Puaray, the modern-day site of the New Mexican town of Santa Fe. Having reached the village, with its three- and four-story pueblos, they were saddened by the news that the two friars they sought had been killed.

Despite their disappointment, Fray Bernardino and Espejo continued their exploration of the Rio Grande region. Like their predecessors, they wandered onto the plains to the east and saw their first bison herds. They returned west to the Rio Grande, crossed the river, and traveled to the Acoma pueblo and others farther west. They visited with Indians who remembered Coronado from 40 years earlier and even found a traveling chest of Coronado's, as well as one of his books.

On their return trip to Mexico, Bernardino and Espejo divided their party and traveled in two separate groups. Espejo and his men followed the Pecos River until they reached the Río de las Vacas (the River of Cows). From information provided by local Natives, Espejo determined that the river flowed into the Rio Grande and that taking this route would lead them to the Conchos River, the way home. During one leg of Espejo's journey, he and his men marched far to the west, to the Zuñi pueblo on the modern-day New Mexico–Arizona border. Here he encountered Indian guides who led him to some remote silver mines. Espejo wrote of his valuable findings: "I found them, and with my own hands, I extracted ore from them, said by those who know to be very rich and to contain much silver."[15] On his return swing eastward, Espejo claimed he discovered additional mines near the Rio Grande from which he extracted lumps of "shining ore."[16]

On August 21, 1583, the military expedition reached the confluence of the Rio Grande and the Conchos, where the travelers had first met the Indians who had informed them of the death of the two priests. When Espejo returned to Mexico, he brought back new information that gave the Spanish authorities a clearer picture of the landscape and river system of modern-day New Mexico. He also suggested that a permanent northern kingdom in the Rio Grande region be established, naming the proposed kingdom New Andalusia.

Despite his recommendations, no new Spanish colony was built in the region. Establishing such colonies was strictly regulated, and the process moved painfully slow through the Spanish bureaucracy, both in Mexico City and in Madrid. Indeed, Spain's King Philip II might take months before he even took a glance at such an application for colonization. Seven years were to pass before another expedition to the region was mounted.

In 1590, the Spanish lieutenant governor of Nuevo León, Gaspar Castano de Sosa, marched 170 of his people, the entire population of the mining village of Almaden, north into New Mexico. Almaden (modern-day Monclova) was located 200 miles south of the juncture of the Pecos River and Rio Grande, just east of the Big Bend. The party was accompanied by a long supply train and two brass cannon. Sosa knew of Espejo's explorations and of the silver he had found west of the Rio Grande. His miners would take up where Espejo had left off. Despite his intentions, however, de Sosa's expedition was unauthorized. Although he managed to reach the Rio Grande and the Pecos River—subjugating along the way the pueblos at Pecos, Taos, and Tiguex—Spanish officials learned of his illegal venture and dispatched a company of soldiers to track him down. Under the command of Captain Juan Marlete, the soldiers arrested Sosa and his entire mining crew, marching them all back south. Sosa would bear the brunt of punishment for his actions. His case landed on the desk of the king in Madrid who ordered that Sosa was to be severely punished. In due course, Sosa was tried, found guilty, and sentenced to exile in China.

Despite the harsh treatment given Sosa for his unauthorized expedition, two other explorers, Captain Francisco Leyva de Bonilla and Captain Antonio Gutierrez de Humana, launched a new unauthorized expedition into the region of the Upper Rio Grande. In 1593, the two Spanish officers and a small garrison of soldiers were dispatched by Spanish officials into the lands of New Mexico to subdue several Indian uprisings. Although their orders were to return after their mission was accomplished,

Leyva and Gutierrez decided to march farther north, taking any men under their command who agreed to accompany them. Some refused, knowing the venture was illegal. The Leyva-Gutierrez expedition pressed northward, but the campaign did not go well.

The party reached the lands of the Pueblo Indians, where they established a base of operation. They then marched to Quivira, possibly reaching the Platte River. Almost from the start, the expedition was marked by violence. The two captains had a falling out, and Gutierrez murdered Leyva. Soon after, Gutierrez and his party were ambushed by Indians. Only one soldier, Alonso Sanchez, survived the attack. He was eventually adopted by an Indian tribe. Several of the party's Indian guides managed to escape. One of these, a Pueblo named Jusepe, returned to his people only to be captured by the Apaches and held captive for a year. He managed to escape, and several years later he related the story of the lost Leyva-Gutierrez expedition to yet another Spanish official who marched into the lands of the Rio Grande. The Spaniard was Juan de Oñate, the man destined to become the true colonizer of New Mexico.

THE COLONIZER OF NEW MEXICO

For years, the assignment of an official expedition and sponsor to colonize the northlands of the Rio Grande had been delayed by red tape, bureaucratic hesitancy, and royal foot dragging. In 1595, however, as the sixteenth century was approaching its end, the Spanish government in Madrid selected a New World official to launch and establish such a colony, a man descended from the house of the great Spanish conqueror of the Aztecs, Hernando Cortés. There were several reasons that Don Juan de Oñate, a longtime resident of the New World, was chosen for the task. In all likelihood, his connection to the great Cortés was probably the least of the reasons. As a military man, Juan de Oñate had fought Indians on the northern borders of

New Spain. He was a personal associate of the governing viceroy, and he was wealthy.

In making his appeal to receive the privilege of establishing a legitimate colony in the northlands, Oñate had offered his personal wealth to be used to build a colony "by peaceful means, friendliness, and Christian zeal."[17] Using his own wealth, he would recruit and organize a party of 200 male colonists and their families. In addition, he promised to purchase 3,000 sheep, 1,000 goats, 1,000 head of cattle, a wide array of needed tools, and 500 pesos worth of "wheat for sowing."[18] To ensure the spiritual life of his colony, Oñate requested that at least six priests accompany his party to the north. These friars would minister to the spiritual needs of the colonists and would convert the local Indians to Catholicism. In return for his investment in New Mexico, Oñate asked to be appointed governor of the new Spanish province, to be given the title *adelantado* (governor or captain-general), and that the title be passed on to two additional generations of his family. He also requested the noble title of marquis and a personal land grant of 30 square leagues of property. These titles and privileges were bestowed upon Oñate from Spain.

Oñate had little trouble recruiting the 200 colonists for his exploration of the Upper Rio Grande. Official delays and a change in viceroys, however, delayed both his plans and grants from the Spanish government. When all obstacles were finally removed, years had passed and Oñate's male recruits had been reduced to 129 by 1598; the long delay having caused much hardship. Many who had provided their own supplies of food for the venture had consumed their stores; Oñate replaced their provisions out of his own pocket. Even before he had set foot in the region of the Upper Rio Grande, the planned colony had cost Oñate more than he had expected.

By late spring of 1598, the Oñate expedition was underway, crossing the scrub brushlands of Chihuahua, bound for the Rio

Grande. As the group embarked, Oñate prematurely laid official claim to lands he had not yet reached. His claim was formal, however, and all encompassing. He declared his possession of all

> lands, pueblos, cities, towns, castles, fortified and unfortified houses which are not established in the kingdoms of and provinces of New Mexico . . . the mountains, rivers, fisheries, waters, pastures, valleys, meadows, springs, and ores of gold, silver, copper, mercury, tin, iron, precious stones, salt . . . with power of life and death, over high and low, from the leaves of the trees to the stones and sands of the [Rio Grande].[19]

Although Oñate was already a wealthy man, he had ambitious dreams of gaining additional wealth from his investment. He was also interested in achieving fame and political power.

When Oñate's party entered New Mexico, 129 soldiers and their families along with 20 missionaries made up the group, a total of nearly 400 people. Oñate was the first Spanish colonizer in the northlands to use wagons; his caravan included 80 wagons, called *carros*, that carried the colonists' supplies and household goods. As his group moved north into the Upper Rio Grande valley of northern New Mexico, they encountered the Pueblo Indians at Acoma. These Natives were unfriendly to Oñate and his party, and he laid siege to the village. The Natives defended themselves by throwing stones from the rooftops of their multistory pueblo complexes, but the Spaniards succeeded in capturing the pueblo. In the bloody aftermath of their victory, they slaughtered 800 men, women, and children. Every Pueblo warrior who survived lost a foot, a cruel form of revenge exacted by the victors. The Acoma massacre was viewed by some in Oñate's party as unnecessary, and the violent encounter appalled them. Because of such actions, they claimed, the Pueblos of the Upper Rio Grande would never be converted to Christianity. Because of the excessive nature of the "battle" and Oñate's forceful, autocratic administration of his party, several of his colonists decided to abandon the mission. Despite the defections, Oñate did establish a site for his colonial capital—which he named San Gabriel—across the river at Yunque. By the summer of 1600, 80 additional colonists joined Oñate's original group, among them seven priests.

Despite the relative successes of Oñate's mission to establish a New Mexican colony, he proved to be the wrong man for the job. The Spanish leader was harsh with his colonists and became obsessed, as Coronado had 60 years earlier, with finding riches and gold. Because of this obsession, Oñate sometimes ignored the needs of people and established a permanent outpost in the wilderness of the Upper Rio Grande. He siphoned field workers and others from important tasks to pursue frivolous ventures to unexplored territory, where one of the legendary Seven Cities of Cíbola might still lie undetected, its riches there for the taking. Many of the colonists and several of the priests decided to abandon the colony and return south to New Spain. When they reported Oñate's faults to Spanish officials—including a lack of conversions, the poverty of the colony, and the repeated threat of starvation—his reign as provincial leader soon came to an end. His mismanagement and harsh treatment of colonists and the Pueblo Indians caused him to be stripped of his titles and power over New Mexico. He was fined 6,000 ducats for his crimes and poor administrative decisions, and was banished from Mexico City for four years.

In his wake, a new leader of New Mexico was selected. Don Pedro de Peralta succeeded Oñate as governor and captain-general, arriving at what remained of the colony in the fall of 1609. To placate the Pueblo Indians, who had never accepted Spanish presence, Peralta moved the site of the New Mexican capital away from the pueblo villages. His new capital, established in 1610, was located farther south and was called

La Villa Real de la Santa Fe de San Francisco. In a short period of time, the colonists began referring to their new settlement site at Santa Fe as "Holy Faith."

For several years, Santa Fe and the New Mexican colony hung on precariously. A census taken in 1617 listed only 48 settlers in the colony. The friars, however, achieved a moderate degree of success. They converted many Pueblo Indians and even encouraged their converts to accept pacification. By 1629, a governor's report to Mexico City cited thousands of conversions among the Pueblos and listed the number of friars working the Upper Rio Grande at 50. (A report for 1631 listed 66 priests.)

The Franciscan friars were essential to the success of many Spanish settlements and colonial enterprises. Spain understood that Native Americans could not be changed or pacified overnight. Typically, the Spanish anticipated the need for ten years of work before many Indian culture groups could be successfully subdued, dominated, and "civilized." The typical settlement pattern for Spanish colonies was to deliver priests to any region that might be suitable for colonization to serve as a vanguard presence. Only later would the Spanish send in significant numbers of middle-class colonists and upper-class aristocrats to rule them.

The Franciscans established their ecclesiastical base at Santo Domingo, located about 30 miles south of present-day Santa Fe. Fanning out across the Rio Grande valley and beyond, these gray-robed, bearded men of God taught the Pueblo Indians a faith that was quite different from their own. Their success can be attributed in part to skillful storytelling. As the Franciscans told colorful stories to the Pueblos, they gradually converted to the Christian faith—by the hundreds and then by the thousands. The Franciscans did not limit their teaching to the Scriptures. Using European tools, they also taught their Indian converts carpentry and masonry. Indian labor was used in the construction of adobe mission churches under the

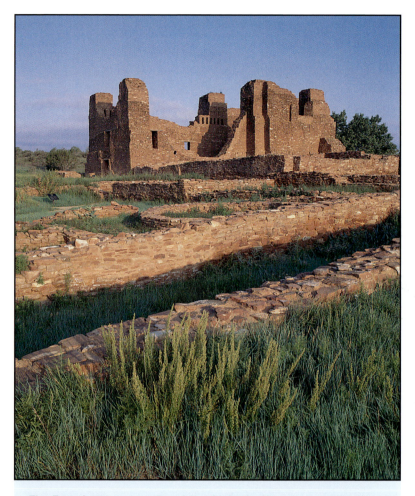

The Franciscans, an order of the Catholic Church, established missions that were designed to indoctrinate local Natives in the ways of the church. Shown here is Quarai Mission, which is located in central New Mexico and is today part of Salinas Pueblo Missions National Monument.

supervision of the Franciscans. As early as 1630, the Franciscan fathers reported to the king of Spain that 50 of their number were busy preaching, teaching, and building in 90 Indian villages and that each of these Indian villages had its own church.

During these crucial years for the New Mexican colony, colonists remained in close contact with Mexico City. From the capital of New Spain, royal caravans arrived in Santa Fe every three years, beginning in 1609. The supply wagons delivered much-needed provisions and articles for the new mission churches, including artwork, candleholders, and other ecclesiastical items. In return, the New Mexican colony sent back raw materials and natural trade goods, such as animal hides, leather, textiles, salt, and other commodities. This exchange, while not frequent, did provide a trade base for Santa Fe beyond barter with local Indians. The arrival of a caravan from the capital was the one regularly scheduled contact the Upper Rio Grande colony had with Mexico City and mainstream Spanish civilization. After a time, a permanent road developed between Santa Fe and Mexico City—*El Camino Real*, or the Royal Road. This treacherous route passed through the difficult terrain of southern New Mexico; with its arid deserts and natural hazards, it was a region the Spaniards came to know as *La Jornada del Muerto*, the Journey of the Dead.

Throughout the seventeenth century, the New Mexican colony developed, took root, and ultimately thrived. It was never without problems, however. There were clashes between the priests of the colony and various governmental leaders as well as a measure of inequality between the churchmen and the lay colonists. Many of the colonists lived in relative poverty. These individuals were sometimes envious of the affluence of the Catholic mission lands, where Pueblo populations were exploited; their labor serving as tribute to the Spanish Crown. Some governors claimed jurisdiction over the church lands and the friars themselves. This caused the priests to complain that such governors were placing their authority and that of the Spanish government above that of the pope.

Friars also complained that some governors were exploiting Native populations for their own personal financial gain.

Several governors became so notorious that they were investigated, replaced, and sometimes jailed or excommunicated by the Catholic Church. One example was Diego de Penalosa, governor of New Mexico from 1661 to 1664, who was brought to trial by the church and found guilty of heresy. He was heavily fined, barred from holding any other public office, and ordered to "march barefoot through the streets of Mexico City while carrying a green candle of penitence."[20]

These clashes between church and state continued throughout much of the seventeenth century; but it was another conflict that finally came to a violent head in the early 1680s that nearly drove the Spanish from New Mexico. Throughout the years of Spanish control over much of the Native population of New Mexico, the indigenous peoples were constantly exploited by the friars and the Spanish royal officials. Sometimes the clashes between the Indians and the church were cultural. In 1675, for example, a friar at the San Ildefonso pueblo charged 47 Indian medicine men with witchcraft. After four of the medicine men were hanged for their alleged crimes, Indian leaders approached the governor for the release of the others, threatening the official if he failed to let them go. The governor relented. One of the 43 Indian holy men released was a Pueblo ironically named Pope. Once freed, Pope began gathering support for a Pueblo uprising against the Spaniards, establishing his recruiting base in Taos, north of Santa Fe. (For additional information on this Pueblo Indian, enter "Pueblo, Pope" into any search engine and browse the many sites listed.)

There was widespread discontent among the region's Native American population, and many were drawn to Pope and his plans for an uprising. In addition to the resentment the Indians harbored toward the Spaniards, several years of recurring drought across New Mexico had killed their crops. As stored supplies of grain were depleted, starvation among the Indians became commonplace.

When word of Pope's plans leaked out, a concerned and frightened friar, Fray Francisco de Ayeta, traveled to Mexico City to raise a military contingent to put down the planned Indian revolt. Before he could return to Santa Fe, the Natives launched the Pueblo Revolt of 1680. At the heart of the revolt was the ongoing exploitation of the Pueblo Indians, who were forced to work for the friars and pay multiple tributes to Spanish officials. The Indians were also inspired to revolt because they had been ordered to bring an end to their Native dances and nature worship, which the friars considered pagan and sacrilegious. Pueblo villages were also being raided by local Navajo and Apache bands, and the Spanish government did little to protect them from these raids.

The Pueblo leader and medicine man, Pope, set August 13, 1680, as the date for the uprising. He sent messenger-runners to all the neighboring pueblos to encourage their inhabitants to rise up and slaughter the local Spanish leaders. Each runner carried "a piece of knotted cord, the number of knots indicating the days remaining before the attack."[21] When two of his runners were caught and revealed their message to Spanish officials, Pope changed the date for the uprising to August 10. In a unified gesture of solidarity and defiance, the Pueblo Indians followed Pope's lead and the revolt began. The Indians moved systematically from village to village, killing Spanish men, women, and children. They were especially brutal with the friars.

The day of the uprising soon revealed how thorough Pope had been in recruiting his fellow Native Americans in the destruction of the Spanish presence in New Mexico:

> All through the day reports flooded in [to Santa Fe]. Pecos, Taos, Santa Cruz, San Marcos, San Cristobal, Santo Domingo, Santa Clara, Picuris—all the pueblos in the area had risen, all the churches were being burned, all the priests killed. As far

away as Acoma and the Zuñi and Hopi villages to the west there was death and destruction. By the night of the 10th, all Spaniards in the Santa Fe area had swarmed into the town. Survivors from the devastated areas to the north and west ran gauntlets of raiding parties to seek safety in Santa Fe.[22]

Santa Fe was protected by a garrison of only 150 soldiers who fought Indians throughout the day in the fields outside the town. By nightfall, more than 1,000 Indians had reached the capital, and the soldiers took refuge inside the town walls. By the following morning, 2,500 Native American combatants had completely surrounded the town. By August 16, they had taken control of every part of the capital except the plaza grounds, setting fire to the buildings until "the whole town became a torch."[23] They cut off the city's water supply by blocking the ditch that delivered water. On August 17, Indian besiegers tormented and mocked the beleaguered Spaniards in Santa Fe by chanting the Catholic liturgy in Latin.

The soldiers in Santa Fe held out against the repeated Indian assaults until August 21, when the Spanish capital of New Mexico was abandoned. As they moved out of town, they followed "the old yellow silk banner that Spanish soldiers had carried into New Mexico the century before."[24] Fleeing south, some Spanish refugees took up residence in the village of El Paso del Norte, a mission town founded just 20 years earlier. Some eventually moved across the Rio Grande and founded a community on the site of present-day El Paso, Texas. (El Paso del Norte is today the Mexican border town of Ciudad Juárez). For the time being, the Spanish operated from their new "capital" at El Paso, which was located within the borders of the province of New Mexico.

Prior to the Indian attacks, the Spanish population of the Upper Rio Grande was approximately 2,800. In all, the Pueblo uprising resulted in the deaths of 400 Spaniards, approximately one out of every seven colonists. Another 400 were missing and presumed dead. Twenty-three friars were killed; only 11 survived. The Pueblos took out their frustration and revenge on the Spanish settlement buildings as well, destroying homes, government buildings, and especially churches. As buildings burned, so did the official records, church documents, and books they held.

By the following year, Spanish military forces had defeated several groups of Pueblo Indians and had managed to bring them under Spanish control. Some pueblo complexes were found abandoned, their residents gone, having fled into the local mountains. New Mexico and the lands of the Upper Rio Grande were retaken after years of long, difficult military campaigns. Even then, the vast majority of the Pueblo Indians who had "converted" to Christianity, an estimated 16,000, remained hostile to the Catholic faith and were opposed to the ongoing presence of the Spaniards in their lands. Those Indians who had been baptized were washed with soapweed to remove the stigma of Christianity. All Christian Indian marriages were no longer binding.

There is an ironic footnote to the history of the Pueblo Revolt. Pope, the leader of the revolt, was soon corrupted by his own success. Even as he ordered the destruction of Spanish churches, ranch haciendas, and government houses, the Indian leader took possession of the governor's palace in Santa Fe as his own, declaring himself governor of all the pueblos. All too soon, other Native Americans were paying tribute to an Indian governor, one who proved to be as harsh a ruler as the Spaniards had ever been.

5

Mexicans and Americans

Throughout the century that followed the 1680 Pueblo Revolt, the Spanish in the Upper Rio Grande valley struggled to recover their hold on the region. They eventually managed not only to reestablish their power over the Pueblos but to extend their dominance even further. The organizer of the uprising, Pope, was dead within a decade of the revolt, and in 1692, the Spanish launched a major military campaign into New Mexico under the command of Don Diego de Vargas. De Vargas laid siege to Santa Fe, driving out the Pueblo Indians who had occupied it for 12 years. Two years later, 700 colonists and soldiers entered Santa Fe. De Vargas' reconquest of the neighboring pueblos continued until 1696. His reports that year claimed that he had subdued all the Pueblo villages, with the exception of Acoma, as well as a handful of Hopi villages.

During the 1700s, the Pueblo Indians remained passive and cooperative, and Spanish colonialism would prove less offensive to the Native Americans of the Upper Rio Grande. The conquerors' treatment of the Indians was less harsh, less autocratic, and more tolerant:

> Spain had abandoned hope of full-scale colonization: it was too expensive and promised too few rewards. The colonists and the Pueblos needed one another to fend off the Apache and the Navajo, and a brisk trade began in selling one another Indian slaves captured from their mutual enemies. The Pueblos were tacitly permitted to practice their own faith alongside Catholicism: church and kiva, [kachinas] and Christ all came to coexist in relative harmony. Colonists and colonized intermarried. The boundaries between the Indian and Spanish worlds had begun to blur.[25]

Although the Spanish government pursued a less aggressive policy in the northlands during the eighteenth century, Spain had by no means abandoned the region. Additional settlements, such as Albuquerque, were established. Governor Francisco Cuervo y Valdez dispatched a Spanish presence there in 1706. Sixty miles south of Santa Fe, the settlement was composed of 30 colonizing families. Farther south, in the Big Bend region of the Rio Grande, Franciscan friars established missions on the north side of the river, where the village of Presidio had recently been established. By 1767, Spanish soldiers were being garrisoned on the south side of the Rio Grande in a fort that would one day become the center of the Mexican border town of Ojinaga. Along the modern-day Texas banks of the Lower Rio Grande, the Spaniards established the civil settlement of Laredo in 1755. Parish churches were established in 1797 in the larger, more prominent Spanish settlements of New Mexico, including Santa Fe, Albuquerque, Santa Cruz de la Canada, and El Paso.

Gradually, the Spanish population in the region increased, passing the 5,000 mark by 1750 and mushrooming to nearly 25,000 by the turn of the nineteenth century. In the meantime, the Pueblo population had fallen to 13,500 by mid-century, largely because of wars with neighboring Navajo and Apache tribes. Smallpox epidemics that spread among Pueblo villages from 1779 to 1780 further reduced their numbers to around 10,000 by 1800. All along the Rio Grande, from New Mexico to the Gulf region, the Spaniards consolidated their presence and interests by establishing ranches and military forts called presidios. By 1773, the presidio system experienced a general overhaul as the Spanish examined where their greatest interests were centered in the region. That same year, the presidio at Huajuquilla was removed to Valle de San Elceario (modern-day San Elizario), just three miles south of present-day Clint, Texas. Halfway between San Carlos and San Elceario, the Spanish built the Presidio de Pilares on the Rio Grande. Special companies of soldiers, called "flying companies," were placed in the region as eighteenth-century special-forces units. Highly mobile, they were theoretically able to travel from one presidio to another whenever the need arose. By 1780, a new presidio was built at San Vicente on the Mexican side of the Rio Grande between Boquillas and Glenn Springs.

The presidios were often little more than frontier fortresses that garrisoned soldiers who were expected to protect Spanish haciendas and Catholic missions. Their presence along the Rio Grande did not last long. By the 1790s, the long-term presence of the Spanish friars and padres was beginning to decline, and several missions along the Rio Grande and the Conchos River were abandoned. By the turn of the century, the old symbols of Spanish colonial life—the religious missions and the scattered military outposts—were falling apart, increasingly ignored by the government in Mexico City, 1,200 miles away. One of the last to disappear was the Del Norte presidio at Ojinaga. Probably garrisoned and abandoned several times during the late 1700s and early 1800s, the presidio came under Apache attack in 1820, resulting in the deaths of nearly every Spanish citizen in the region.

By 1800, the Spanish had occupied various regions of the Rio Grande for more than 250 years. They had established toehold settlements (including garrisons and presidios), villages and mission outposts, ranches, roads, and trails. By the end of the eighteenth century, however, the period of Spanish colonial dominance, not only in the northlands of the Rio Grande but of New Spain itself (modern-day Mexico), was about to end. In the early morning hours of September 16, 1810, the Mexican people rose up in revolt against their Spanish overlords. The revolt began in the village of Dolores, 200 miles north of Mexico City. The revolution quickly spread—the number of those involved in the uprising reaching almost 100,000. In 1813, a rebel army marched into the city of Acapulco and declared Mexico an independent state, free from Spanish control.

On the brink of success, the insurrection began to fall apart. Spaniards, including the *creoles* (people of Spanish descent born in the New World) and *peninsulares* (people born in Spain), banded together against the Indians and *mestizos* (persons of Spanish and Indian descent). By 1820, infighting among various elements of the revolution allowed Spanish forces to regain control of nearly all the towns, cities, and rural lands the revolutionaries had managed to capture. Nevertheless, extraordinary change was to take place in Mexico during the following year. A liberal movement in Spain forced King Ferdinand VII to accept constitutional law and reduced royal power. Ironically, those who had fought against the revolution in Mexico the previous year, the political conservatives, turned against the Spanish monarchy and launched their own revolt. By February 1821, a coalition of various groups agreed on a new plan of government for Mexico's future, one that called for Mexican independence from Spain, the establishment of a new constitutional monarchy in Mexico City, and equality for all Mexican people. After centuries of Spanish repression, Mexico was finally rid of Spain and the country was on the verge of becoming the Republic of Mexico.

These changes taking place more than 1,000 miles from the waters of the Rio Grande would have a ripple effect that would ultimately change the history of the northlands from New Mexico to Texas. However, sweeping change did not come overnight. Life in these lands, situated so far from the former Spanish and now Mexican capital of Mexico City, had often followed its own course and its own rhythm, both culturally and politically. By the early decades of the nineteenth century, as Mexico faced rebellion and political change, the New Mexican provincial town of Santa Fe was marking its two hundredth anniversary as the region's commercial hub. With a population of more than 4,000 "citizens of Spanish blood,"[26] Santa Fe had developed into a thriving capital of frontier commerce, where residents traded with Indians, as they had for centuries, and soon began to trade with another group of Westerners—Anglo-Americans.

The earliest Americans to reach the Rio Grande and New Mexico came in small groups that were simply passing through the region. Anglo-American fur trappers and hunters reached Presidio del Norte for the first time in 1800. After the U.S. government purchased the vast Louisiana Territory from the French in 1803, however, New Mexico suddenly found itself sharing a border with the United States. Almost immediately, there were border disputes, and any official U.S. presence in the vicinity of New Mexico was considered an act of either aggression or espionage. The U.S. government-sponsored expedition of Lieutenant Zebulon Pike into the province of New Mexico in 1806–07 was a case in point.

TRADE ALONG THE SANTA FE TRAIL

The break between Spain and Mexico also signaled other changes for the former Spanish-controlled provinces of the Rio Grande. Before the success of the 1821 conservative revolution in Mexico, foreign trade in the Spanish provinces of the north was strictly forbidden. Outsiders were looked upon skeptically and were generally unwelcome. A group of American entrepreneurs, led by Robert McKnight, entered Santa Fe in 1812, believing the Spanish ban on U.S. trade had ended. Unaware that the revolution of 1810 had failed, they were quickly arrested. Their trade goods were confiscated, and they were moved to Mexico City where they were thrown into prison. There they remained until the successful revolution of 1821.

The year 1821 also witnessed the establishment of trade between the Mexicans in Santa Fe and American traders from Missouri. That summer, New Mexican buffalo hunters met up with a group of Missouri traders led by William Becknell of Franklin, Missouri. The New Mexicans informed the Americans that Santa Fe was open for their business. This caused Becknell

(continued on page 62)

THE EXPEDITION OF ZEBULON PIKE

Following the U.S. purchase of the western territory of Louisiana in 1803, the Spanish were introduced to a new neighbor to the north—the United States. It did not take long before Spanish officials in Santa Fe and a U.S. expedition of explorers found themselves in the midst of a potential international incident.

At the same time that U.S. President Thomas Jefferson dispatched the famous team of Meriwether Lewis and William Clark up the Missouri River to explore the vast, uncharted lands of the American West, a U.S. general in St. Louis, James Wilkinson, sent another explorer west—Zebulon Pike. Pike was a young military officer who had been assigned to various military outposts in the West. His first mission was to follow the Mississippi River to its source. After eight months on the river, he returned to St. Louis in the spring of 1806 after having reached what he thought were the headwaters of the river. (He had actually missed the source completely.)

General Wilkinson then sent Pike in a different direction—across Louisiana Territory. After delivering 51 Osage Indians to their homeland in western Missouri, the army officer/explorer proceeded to modern-day Nebraska, Kansas, and Colorado. Here, the border between the United States and the northern provinces of Spain was not yet clearly defined. Spanish officials in Santa Fe had received word that the Americans were making contact with Indian tribes they considered loyal to them and dispatched 600 Spanish soldiers to the Great Plains to intercept Pike.

By November 1806, Pike had reached the vicinity of modern-day Colorado Springs. (It was here that Pike named a mountain peak in the Rocky Mountains after himself, the well-known Pike's Peak.) Pushing his men farther south, Pike reached the Sangre de Cristo Range of south-central Colorado and northern New Mexico. Although Pike was fully aware he was trespassing on Spanish soil, he continued. Soon he was met by a detachment of 100 Spanish cavalrymen under the command of Bartolome Fernandez. Pike pretended he was lost, but Fernandez did not believe him. Pike and his men were arrested and taken to the provincial capital of Santa Fe.

Spanish authorities in Santa Fe were uncertain what to do with Pike. They were concerned that his military expedition was a spy mission;

scouting out Spanish territory for possible acquisition by the United States. The local governor, Joaquin del Rael Alencaster, ordered Pike to surrender all his papers and journals, including any maps. Although Pike tried to keep his papers out of the governor's hands by distributing them among his men, nearly all of them were discovered and confiscated. (Pike managed to conceal one journal by rolling up the papers and hiding them in the barrel of a gun.) Eventually, despite Alencaster's initial paranoia, he became friends with Pike and treated him well. In time, the American explorer was released with his men; they returned to St. Louis in 1807.

Pike later wrote about his travels in Louisiana Territory and of his time spent in Santa Fe and other Spanish settlements. He published his manuscript (much of it compiled from memory) in 1810. Pike had been impressed by what he had seen and described the scenes and people he had encountered in New Mexico in glowing terms:

> The water of the Rio Grande fertilized the plains and fields which border its banks on both sides, and we saw men, women and children of all ages and sexes at the joyful labor which was to crown with rich abundance their future harvest and insure them plenty for the ensuing year. . . . Their remote situation also causes them to exhibit in a superior degree the heaven-like qualities of hospitality and kindness in which they appear to endeavor to fulfill the injunction of the scripture.*

Pike's popular book managed to have a greater impact on history than his expedition. After reading about the beautiful landscape of the Southwest and about the opportunities it might afford outsiders, many Americans set their sights on the Mexican frontier.

Pike did not live long after his explorations into the lands of New Mexico and the Upper Rio Grande. He was killed in 1813 during service in the War of 1812. As for his confiscated journals, they were rediscovered a century later in Mexico City, found by a historian doing research in Mexico's archives.

* Time-Life, 141.

Best known for discovering the Colorado peak that bears his name, U.S. Army Lieutenant Zebulon Pike explored the southwestern region of Louisiana Territory in the early 1800s. In 1810, Pike published an account of his expedition that detailed the weakness of Spanish authority in New Mexico and the benefits of trading with Mexico.

(continued from page 59)

and his men to make a detour to the Southwest with their trade goods (they had originally intended to trade with Plains Indians), cross the Sangre de Cristo Mountains, slip through Raton Pass along the Colorado–New Mexican border, and enter the provincial capital. Displaying their manufactured wares in the streets of Santa Fe, the Americans were welcomed, and they soon walked away with significant profits. (One trader bartered his $60 worth of trade goods for $900 in Spanish gold and silver.) When Becknell and his men returned to Missouri, their story inspired others to follow in their wake the following year.

The traders who traveled across the Southwest from Missouri to New Mexico followed a land route they soon named the Santa Fe Trail. The trade that developed between the two countries because of this trail proved mutually beneficial to both the Americans and the residents of New Mexico. In the past, trade connections with Mexico City had always been tenuous and unreliable, as well as limited in scope. It had always taken five months to cover the 1,000-plus miles south along the Turquoise Trail from Santa Fe just to Chihuahua. Any American trade goods that had previously entered Santa Fe had come from Mexico after arriving at the only legal port of entry—Veracruz. Furthermore, trade goods had been slowly shipped north to New Mexico in old, creaky cottonwood carts. By the time these lumbering carts had reached the streets of the New Mexican capital, even the cheapest goods they carried were expensive, the long journey causing "calico [to be] sold for two or three dollars a yard."[27] Now the Americans were delivering manufactured goods, including furniture, tableware, oil lamps, medicines, inks, and paints as well as agricultural products such as tobacco, spices, foodstuffs, and wines. Because the route was better, the goods arrived more quickly. Because they arrived more quickly, they were more affordable.

To deliver his trade goods to Santa Fe, Becknell enlisted the heavy but durable Conestoga wagons made in eastern Pennsylvania. These large, scooped-end wagons could carry a great number of trade items and held up well. Becknell noted how well the wagons were suited to the Santa Fe Trail: "No where else on the American continent can be found a route of 800 miles in extent more easily traversed by wagons than the one between Independence and Santa Fe."[28]

Throughout the 1820s and into the 1830s, the Santa Fe Trail trade served as a conduit for American infiltration into the Mexican regions of the Upper Rio Grande. Missouri wagons arrived annually with greater amounts of trade goods. In 1824, 25 wagons carrying $35,000 worth of American goods arrived in a large caravan from Missouri. Those goods sold for nearly $200,000 in gold and silver or other bartered goods. By the late 1820s, the trail trade generated nearly $1 million in business between the United States and Mexico. For most of a generation, the citizens of Santa Fe were thrilled at the arrival of the Americans and their stores-on-wheels. As the Missouri traders entered the town's streets, according to one eyewitness, excitement greeted the foreign traders:

> Native cries of "Los Americanos! Los Carros! La entrada de la Caravana!" were to be heard in every direction, and crowds of women and boys flocked around to see the newcomers. The wagoners were by no means free from excitement on this occasion. Each one must tie a brand new cracker to the lash of his whip, for on driving them through the streets every one strives to outshine his comrades in the dexterity with which he flourishes his favorite badge of authority.[29]

In time, the trail became a "two-way street"[30] with Mexican pack trains of Spanish mules following the trail northeastward to Missouri where they traded in the streets of St. Louis and Independence just as American traders bartered their goods in the dusty streets of Santa Fe. So many Spanish mules were used on the trail and traded to Missourians that the animal became an American symbol—the Missouri mule.

MOUNTAIN MEN AND FUR TRAPPERS

The Santa Fe Trail trade provided opportunities for Americans to enter the exotic world of New Mexico and the Upper Rio Grande. Another form of business, trade, and occupation brought additional outsiders into the region. During the 1820s and '30s, the wide-open spaces of the American West drew a new type of entrepreneur into New Mexico—the mountain man and the fur trapper.

Fur had proved a vital trade commodity in other parts of North America in earlier eras; and now fur—especially beaver fur—became the center of an extraordinary trade system throughout the Rocky Mountain region, including the Sangre de Cristo range of the southern Rockies. Three significant fur trading centers developed in the American West during the early 1800s. The British operated out of Fort Vancouver in the Pacific Northwest, on the lower Columbia River, where the Hudson's Bay Company established a trading post in 1824. The Americans operated out of St. Louis, on the Mississippi River. The center of the Spanish and Mexican fur trade empire was Taos, a small settlement less than 100 miles north of Santa Fe, not far from the banks of the Rio Grande.

Foreigners who had attempted to enter the province of New Mexico to trade on the Santa Fe Trail before the end of Spanish control in 1821 were dealt with harshly. Now, Americans who were caught engaging in the fur trade received equally harsh treatment. Spanish law required that a license be issued to anyone who hunted beaver in New Mexico and such licenses were issued only to permanent residents. American trappers to the region of the Upper Rio Grande paid bribes to Spanish officials to get licenses, a better bargain than suffering the consequences of being caught trading without a license.

Not every outsider was able to corrupt New Mexican officials. Those who could not traded and trapped illegally. Those who reached New Mexico from the Great Plains were sometimes

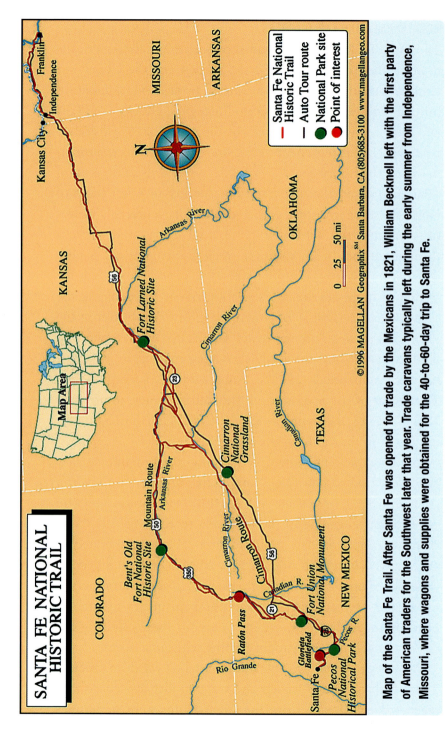

Map of the Santa Fe Trail. After Santa Fe was opened for trade by the Mexicans in 1821, William Becknell left with the first party of American traders for the Southwest later that year. Trade caravans typically left during the early summer from Independence, Missouri, where wagons and supplies were obtained for the 40-to-60-day trip to Santa Fe.

caught by Spanish cavalry patrols, marched down the Rio Grande to El Paso, and placed in prisons in the Spanish province of Chihuahua. Several fur trappers were caught in Chihuahua in 1817, where they were placed in irons and spent most of two months in a Santa Fe jail. Upon their release, the unwanted Americans were relieved of trade goods, supplies, and furs valued at $30,000.

Much of this cat-and-mouse game between outside trappers and Spanish officials came to an end in 1821 as Mexicans took control of their own political future. By the early 1820s, American fur men were to be found in the southern and central Rocky Mountains in search of beaver. Taos had become a convenient supply town, and American traders and trappers were soon populating the streets of Taos and Santa Fe. Thus, during the 1820s, Santa Fe was a bustling trade town, filled with Missourians who had traveled south along the Sante Fe Trail and by mountain fur trappers and traders. Some mountain men used the Rio Grande, floating its length out of the southern Rockies to Santa Fe and sometimes even to El Paso.

A War over
the Rio Grande

In the years following the successful revolution of Mexico against the Spanish, the history of the Rio Grande valley took a decisive turn. Since the northern provinces had always been underpopulated and undercolonized by the Spanish, the new Mexican government opened up Mexico's borderlands, including Texas, to immigrants. Beckoned by the lure of cheap land in Texas, thousands of Americans crossed the border and received generous land grants from the Mexican government. By the 1830s, alarmed at the number of Americans living in a Mexican province, the leaders in Mexico City attempted to close Texas from further colonization and impose stricter control over Americans already living there. In 1835, the Texans revolted and managed to free the province from Mexican control, and in 1845, Texas became the twenty-eighth state to enter the Union.

The annexation of Texas, which was enacted by a congressional resolution, greatly increased the size of the United States, but the move also led to war with Mexico. Bad blood that had already marked the strained relations between the United States and Mexico erupted into a shooting war that unfolded along the banks of the Rio Grande in 1846. The Mexican government had never accepted the independence of Texas, proclaimed in 1836, and an effort to reconquer Texas had been launched in 1841. When that effort failed, Mexican President Antonio López de Santa Anna, who had been defeated during the Texas rebellion of 1835–1836, delivered a stern warning to the United States that the annexation of Texas would precipitate a war between the two countries. (For additional information on this Mexican general and president, enter "Antonio López de Santa Anna" into any search engine and browse the many sites listed.)

In fact, even before the Texas convention voted to accept the offer of U.S. statehood, the U.S. Department of War was preparing to dispatch a field force to the border between Texas and Mexico to ensure that the Mexicans remained at arm's length. The preparation came on the heels of failed diplomatic attempts by U.S. President James K. Polk, who had campaigned for the White House the previous year with a promise to annex Texas. Polk sent a diplomat, John Slidell, to Mexico City to discuss the annexation of Texas and other issues separating Mexico and the U.S. Slidell went to Mexico with orders from Polk to convince the Mexican government to agree to make the Rio Grande the border between Texas and Mexico. An army led by General Zachary Taylor, a 61-year-old Indian fighter from Kentucky, was dispatched to the banks of the Nueces River, the traditional southwestern border of Texas.

Mexican officials refused to meet with Slidell, and by January 12, 1846, President Polk received word from Slidell that negotiations would not take place. The following day, the president ordered a naval blockade of Mexican Gulf ports and instructed General Taylor to move his army to the eastern banks of the Rio Grande. In doing so, Taylor was taking up positions on soil claimed by the Mexican government.

Polk's orders to Taylor were less than clear: If the Mexican government or military made "any open act of hostility toward us, you will not act merely on the defensive."[31] Taylor's army reached the Rio Grande on March 28 and established Fort Texas along the river so that the Americans could observe the Mexicans positioned across the river at Matamoros. Taylor ordered "several wagon tongues spliced together to form a flagstaff and the Star-Spangled Banner was hoisted."[32] Both armies rolled cannon into place within range of one another across the Rio Grande.

The local Mexican commander, Pedro de Ampudia, delivered a stern warning to Taylor two weeks later, informing the U.S. general the Mexicans would attack if Taylor's men remained on Mexican soil. Taylor responded by ordering a naval blockade at the mouth of the Rio Grande to prevent supplies from being delivered upriver to Ampudia's men. On April 25, Mexican General Mariano Arista arrived at Matamoros with

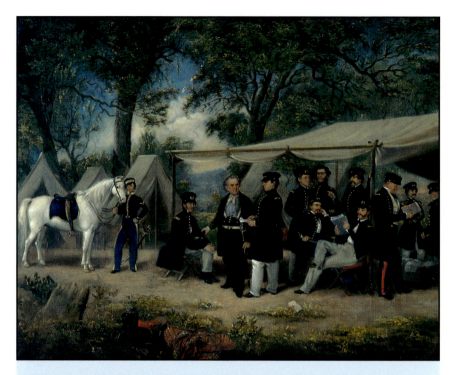

U.S. General Zachary Taylor (center) was sent to the Texas-Mexico border in 1846 to command the U.S. Army against Mexico after the United States had annexed Texas. Under Taylor's command, the United States won key battles at Palo Alto, Monterrey, and Buena Vista, and Taylor would go on to become our nation's twelfth president thanks to his success in helping lead the United States to victory over Mexico.

reinforcements—an army of 2,000 soldiers joined those already in place.

Nearly 11,000 men were now facing one another from opposite banks of the Rio Grande; 8,000 of them were Mexican. The face-off between the Americans and the Mexicans was escalating to an alarming level. The following days brought the two sides to war.

As early as April 23, the Mexican Congress had approved a proclamation for a "defensive war" with the United States. This defensive war began on May 3 when the Americans at Fort Texas came under assault as Mexican cannon fire began blasting their location. The majority of Taylor's forces, including the general himself, were not at Fort Texas that day. They had been dispatched to Point Isabel, about 25 miles downriver at the mouth of the Rio Grande.

For more than five days, the Mexicans rained shot and shell over Fort Texas. Most of the cannonballs fell short of the fort and only two U.S. soldiers were killed, including the commanding officer, Major Jacob Brown. (Brownsville, Texas, a city on the Rio Grande, was later named in his honor.)

The return of General Taylor and his troops brought the bombardment to an end. On May 8, Taylor's forces and the main column of Arista's army faced one another directly at Palo Alto. A battle raged throughout the day across a mile-long front. U.S. cannoneering proved deadly, costing the Mexicans many casualties and resulting in the retreat of the Mexican forces. The artillery exchange also caused a prairie-grass fire that spread quickly across the battlefield, engulfing the grounds where the wounded lay, burning some of the men alive. After two days of fighting, U.S. casualties amounted to 200 men; but the Mexicans suffered losses more than three times that number. The opening shots of the Mexican-American War had been fired.

Even before President Polk received word of the engagements between Taylor and the Mexican Army, he was preparing to request a declaration of war from Congress. On May 9, he met with his cabinet, informing the secretaries that the United States "had ample cause of war."[33] By the time war was declared by Congress on May 11, the fighting was already underway. Polk immediately called for 20,000 American volunteers. In Polk's home state of Tennessee, more than 30,000 men answered the call.

By May 18, however, Taylor's forces had already crossed the Rio Grande and captured the evacuated river town. By the end of June 1846, an army of 12,000 volunteers and regular forces had reached the army outpost at Matamoros. That month, heavy rains caused the Rio Grande to flood, and the battlefield at Palo Alto became a huge, shallow lake filled with catfish.

The U.S. war strategy, planned by the superior commander of all U.S. forces, General Winfield Scott, a veteran of the War of 1812, was a three-pronged attack across the Rio Grande, which included General Taylor's crossing of the river. Another crossing was ordered to take place at Santa Fe. The military force that eventually marched into the Upper Rio Grande region moved out of Fort Leavenworth, Kansas, in June, under the command of an army colonel named Stephen Watts Kearny, another veteran of the War of 1812.

Kearny's field command, the Army of the West, included 1,700 men, and Kearny was promoted to brigadier general during his march across the Southwest to Santa Fe. During this march, Kearny and his men followed the old Santa Fe Trail. Along the way, Kearny learned that a shipment of two wagons loaded with guns purchased in St. Louis was on its way to Santa Fe to help arm the Mexicans. He sent two companies of dragoons (cavalry troops) ahead to intercept the wagons, but they never caught up with them.

Kearny's forces moved quickly along the trail covering the stretch from Independence, Missouri, to Bent's Fort (near present-day La Junta, Colorado) in less than one month. As they reached New Mexico, the U.S. force was met with little or no resistance in villages along their way. In the meantime, New Mexican Governor Manuel Armijo was calling his people to resist the U.S. invasion: "Let us be comrades in arms. . . . Rest assured that your governor is willing and ready to sacrifice his life and all his interests in the defense of his country."[34] As the Americans advanced closer to Santa Fe, Kearny sent messengers ahead with a proclamation to inform the Mexicans at Santa Fe of his coming and to encourage them to lay down their arms. His words began with an invitation to the Mexicans to end the conflict and live peacefully, but they firmly spelled out the consequences of continued armed conflict:

> We come amongst you as friends, not as enemies; we come to you as protectors, not as conquerors; we come amongst you for your benefit, not for your injury. Henceforth, I absolve you from all allegiance to the Mexican government, and from all obedience to General Armijo. He is no longer your governor. I am your governor. I shall not expect you to take up arms, and follow me, to fight against your own people, who may be in arms against me; but I tell you now that those who remain peaceably at home, attending to their herds, shall be protected by me in their property, their persons, and their religion, and not a pepper or an onion shall be disturbed or taken by my troops, without pay or without the consent of the owner! But Listen! He who is found in arms against me I will hang.[35]

Despite Kearny's reassurance of peace, between 3,000 and 4,000 New Mexicans took up defensive positions in Apache Canyon, a narrow pass just 12 miles east of Santa Fe, preparing to meet the Americans in battle. Their positions left Kearny in a difficult spot. If his men advanced into the canyon, they might have been picked off one by one and the situation could have resulted in a bloodbath. The only other alternative was to steer around the canyon, following old narrow mountain trails. Fortunately, the standoff was defused when Kearny's men advanced toward Apache Canyon only to be informed that Armijo had fled to Chihuahua, leaving the town of Santa Fe defenseless.

The following fall, those who had remained in Santa Fe issued a report to the president of Mexico, harshly criticizing Armijo. After he had led thousands of his people to Apache Canyon for the defense of Santa Fe, he had panicked and sent them home. The report continued:

... as soon as the citizenry retired, instead of advancing he and the dragoons and artillery retreated. ... As a result, the troops of the United States occupied this city on August 18 without the slightest resistance ... Sr. Armijo ... can say full well: I have lost everything, including his honor." [36]

Following his bloodless capture of Santa Fe, Kearny remained in the city for a full month. During those weeks, he organized a new ruling government and appointed an American—Charles Bent from Taos—as the civil governor until a new territorial government could be formed. He ordered the drafting of a new civil law code, which was partially based on traditional Spanish principles. Kearny sent a report to President Polk, informing the president that he had established and "secured order" in New Mexico.[37] Despite Kearny's efforts, however, all was not well in the region of the Upper Rio Grande.

When Kearny and his dragoons left Santa Fe, bound for new campaigns in California, they left behind Missouri volunteer units under the command of Colonel Alexander W. Doniphan. The Mexican population resented having U.S. troops in New Mexico, and the situation was made worse when some of the U.S. soldiers used racial slurs and treated non-Anglos with disrespect. This behavior caused some New Mexicans to turn on their occupiers. By year's end, a plot to assassinate Governor Bent was brought to light. Although the conspirators were arrested, Bent remained in harm's way. The following month, January 1847, New Mexican and Pueblo rebels began killing Americans. Governor Bent, who was found while visiting his home in Taos, was also killed. The rebels focused their rage on Bent alone, leaving the women and children in the home unharmed. The governor's body was shot through with arrows as well as bullets. While still alive, Bent was scalped.

Across New Mexico, similar uprisings occurred. During their raids, the rebels set fire to buildings and businesses owned by

Americans in the territory. As Colonel Sterling Price, a local U.S. military officer, observed, the rebels appeared intent on putting "to death every American and every Mexican who had accepted office under the American government."[38] Ultimately, Price was forced to lead five companies of U.S. troops against the rebels, encountering hundreds in skirmishes during a march to Taos in late January. By February 3, Colonel Price arrived at the Taos pueblo, a 300-year-old adobe town where 700 rebels and their families had taken up defensive refuge. After opening a cannon barrage against the pueblo, Price led an infantry assault against the rebel stronghold, killing 150 men. The survivors surrendered and following a speedy trial of the leaders of the uprising, U.S. authorities hanged six rebels.

Before the uprisings had completely run their course, hundreds of New Mexicans would be killed in revolts at Santa Cruz, Mora, Las Vegas, and El Brazito. As the resistance was quelled and rebel leaders were killed or captured, all significant challenges to the U.S. presence in New Mexico had come to an end.

The U.S. military found success at nearly every turn during the Mexican-American War. Kearny, successful in taking control of New Mexico, advanced farther west into California where he helped wrest the coastal region from Mexican hands—not, however, before he had lost a significant skirmish at San Pascual.

Despite the success of such U.S. military leaders as Kearny and others in New Mexico, Arizona, and California, the campaigns in Mexico's northern provinces would have been nothing without the success of General Winfield Scott's army in Mexico. Two months after Kearny and others had subdued California, General Scott landed 10,000 men in the Mexican port city of Veracruz. Six months later, on September 13, 1847, Scott's army occupied Mexico City. With the capture of the Mexican capital and the defeat of the Mexican president,

A painting of the landing of U.S. troops under the command of General Winfield Scott at Veracruz, Mexico, March 1847. Within six months of the landing, the U.S. Army occupied Mexico City and had defeated the Mexicans. As a result of the victory over Mexico, the United States was able to purchase the area that today encompasses California, Arizona, New Mexico, Utah, and Nevada, as well as part of Colorado.

General Santa Anna, negotiations to end the war by formal treaty soon followed.

The peace document, known as the Treaty of Guadalupe Hidalgo, would have a direct impact on the Rio Grande. Concluded and signed on February 2, 1848, the treaty did not call for the annexation of Mexico, as some Americans were hoping. It did, however, force the Mexican government to allow the U.S. government to purchase the northern border-lands, including the lands from California in the West to New Mexico in the East. Prior to the war, the United States had offered to purchase this same region, but Mexico had refused to sell. With the successful conclusion of the war, the United States was able to buy the borderlands for $15 million. (Altogether,

(continued on page 80)

THE RIO GRANDE: A DISPUTED BORDER

Although the Rio Grande is accepted today as the primary border between the United States and Mexico, the river has historically been a source of multiple border disputes and controversies. Almost from the time it was first discovered by Europeans, the Rio Grande has been claimed as a border by rival Old World powers and New World countries. It has also been the source of conflict between individual Mexican and American states. The history of the river and its role as a border is complicated, one full of twists and turns, much like the river itself.

As early as 1525, King Charles V of Spain had designated the Rio Grande (then known by Spain as the Rio de las Palmas) as the western boundary line of the vast Spanish holding of provincial Florida. During the 1680s, when French explorer Robert Cavelier, Sieur de La Salle, arrived in the region of modern-day Texas, he claimed the Rio Grande as the western boundary of his new French colony. An additional French claim to the Rio Grande as a colonial border came in 1716 when explorer Louis Juchereau de Saint Denis urged the French government to promote the Rio Grande as a French borderline. In the early nineteenth century, the French government under Napoleon Bonaparte declared the Rio Grande to be the western border of the Louisiana Territory, which the U.S. government would agree to purchase in 1803. When the purchase was completed, then-president Thomas Jefferson accepted the river as a new U.S. border.

This claim remained on paper only until 1819 when representatives of the U.S. government met with Spanish officials to discuss the transfer of ownership of Florida to the United States. Through the Treaty of 1819, U.S. diplomat John Quincy Adams surrendered any claim to the Rio Grande as a border of Florida "forever." That part of the treaty was unpopular with American expansionists, and various leaders in Congress, including Kentucky Congressman Henry Clay, continued to promote the Rio Grande as a U.S. border. Such claims, however, remained unofficial and pointless. All of Texas was at that time still the property of Spain.

After the opening of the territory of Texas by the newly created Mexican government in the early 1820s, the issue of the Rio Grande as a border again became a topic of debate. With the great influx of American colonists into Mexican-controlled Texas, both sides argued whether the Rio Grande was the border between the Mexican provinces of Texas and Coahuila. While the Americans insisted that the border between the two provinces was the Rio Grande, Mexicans insisted that the western border of Texas was the Nueces River. In 1832 and 1833, American Texans held two statehood conventions, each claiming that the Rio Grande was the one true border of West Texas. Also in 1833, President Andrew Jackson attempted to purchase Texas from the Mexican government, with the Rio Grande as the accepted border. Mexico not only refused to sell its northern province but refused to accept the Rio Grande as the border.

The issue of the Rio Grande and its border status peaked during the Texas Revolution. By 1836, the Texans had defeated the Mexican General Antonio López de Santa Anna in the Battle of San Jacinto, and Texas soon declared its independence. As part of the terms of the treaty forced upon the captured Santa Anna, the Mexican leader accepted the Rio Grande as the border between his defeated country and the new Republic of Texas. Despite the general's acquiescence, the treaty was never ratified by the Mexican Congress, and Santa Anna himself repudiated it following his release by the Texans.

It would take a dramatic and bloody war between the United States and Mexico to settle the centuries-old controversy of the Rio Grande's border status once and for all. An American historian summed up the longstanding dispute:

> In the early summer of 1848, what so long a sequence of claims had labored over and over to effect was now conformed by overwhelming power: that the southeasterly Rio Grande had always seemed a natural boundary between different sovereignties, kings of country and type of society. . . . The Rio Grande in Colorado and New Mexico, and its left bank in Texas, belonged to the United States.*

* Horgan, vol. 2, 781.

(continued from page 77)

these lands included modern-day California, Arizona, New Mexico, Utah, and Nevada, as well as part of Colorado. Land previously claimed by Texas, including the territory between the Nueces River and the Rio Grande, was also included.) Also prior to the war, the Mexican government and the Republic of Texas had each laid claim to the lands between the Nueces River and the Rio Grande. With the terms of the Treaty of Guadalupe Hidalgo, the question of the Rio Grande as a border was settled.

Within two generations, the region that had been under Spanish domination for three centuries had experienced a dramatic power shift with the removal of Spanish authority and the establishment of a Mexico in the hands of the Mexican people. Although transfer from Spanish authority to Mexican control did produce some governmental policy changes, overall, the transition did not result in extraordinary changes in the lives and livelihood of the indigenous population of Spanish-speaking residents. With the success of the Americans in the Mexican-American War and the acquisition of the vast territory of the Southwest from Mexico by the U.S. government, however, the region of the Rio Grande was poised for tremendous change. The era of the Anglo-Americans was about to begin.

7

The Americans Arrive

The arrival of the Americans to the Rio Grande valley coincided with the arrival of the midpoint of the nineteenth century—1850. For the next 60 or 70 years, the region experienced dramatic changes—political, ethnic, social, and economic. Once the Americans took control of the Rio Grande valley, from New Mexico to Texas, the redirecting of the landscape and its people would never end. Despite the arrival of increasing numbers of Anglo-Americans, those of Hispanic blood never completely abandoned the lands their ancestors had occupied for centuries. Although some people of Spanish-Mexican heritage did pack up and move south across the Rio Grande following the signing of the Treaty of Guadalupe Hidalgo, the vast majority did not; neither did the Native Americans who had preceded them in the region. Nonetheless, the days of Indian, Spanish, and Mexican dominance along the Rio Grande had finally come to an end. From 1850 onward, the future of the Rio Grande, at least along the river's northern banks, belonged to the United States.

The Americans wasted little time reorganizing the politics of the Rio Grande region. There were initial clashes, however, over the geopolitical claims of the U.S. government and the state of Texas. The Treaty of Guadalupe Hidalgo had established the Rio Grande as the Mexico-Texas border from the Gulf of Mexico to El Paso. The government of Texas, however, also claimed that this border continued along the Rio Grande to its headwaters, to the forty-second parallel in modern-day Colorado as well as along the Arkansas River. This claim extended Texas into territory "never a part of Texas during Spanish or Mexican rule."[39] For this reason, the Treaty of Guadalupe Hidalgo, which was signed on February 2, 1848, and ratified by the U.S. Senate on March 10, was both a cause for celebration and disappointment to the Texans. That same month, Texas created a new county, Santa Fe County, which extended the state's northwestern boundary across eastern New Mexico, a move designed

The United States and Mexico signed the Treaty of Guadalupe Hidalgo on February 2, 1848, bringing the Mexican-American War to a close. Under the terms of the treaty, Mexico gave up its rights to Texas and ceded 1,193,061 square miles of land in the Southwest to the United States in return for $15 million.

to ensure and define Texas' claim to the northern Rio Grande valley. The Texans sent an emissary, Spruce M. Baird, to Santa Fe to organize the new county.

The people of New Mexico, especially those in Santa Fe, were opposed to the formation of this new county. The local population, including those stationed with the military, were against the move, and Baird found them uncooperative. The local U.S. military commander informed Baird that he intended to hold control over the New Mexican territory established by Stephen Kearny and would do so "at every peril."[40] The U.S. stance on this issue was in direct conflict with the wishes of the non-Anglo population. After several months in the territory, Baird's mission appeared hopeless, and he returned to Texas.

In November 1848, the citizens of Santa Fe held a convention and adopted petitions that were forwarded to Washington, D.C., asking for New Mexico to be made an official territory, a step necessary for eventual statehood. Over the following year, the tension between the residents of New Mexico and the government of Texas continued to escalate. Late in 1849, Texas Governor George T. Wood took a more aggressive stance and proposed to the Texas State Legislature that the time had come for Texas to push its claim to New Mexico "with the whole power and resources of the state."[41] There was even talk of Texas sending in state troops to occupy the region of the Upper Rio Grande. In the meantime, the people of New Mexico held a convention during which they planned to adopt a new state constitution and delineate their claim to the disputed territory. The New Mexicans even redefined their proposed state's territory to include some territory that was unquestionably Texan. By 1850, the issues between New Mexico and Texas over the future of the northern Rio Grande finally came to a head.

That year, the U.S. Congress finally settled the question of eastern New Mexico's independence from Texas. As part of a compromise allowing California to enter the Union as a free state (one not allowing slavery), Congress included several passages relative to the New Mexico–Texas question. In exchange for Texas' support of the compromise, Congress paid Texas $10 million, established the western border of Texas that exists today, and accepted the organization of the territory of New Mexico. While many Texans were opposed to these clauses in the compromise bill, it signaled the end of the border question. As one Texas newspaper observed, "[It is] doubtful whether ten years' trading would give Texas a better bargain than she can now make."[42] On November 25, 1850, the governor of Texas signed the documents that enacted the changes proposed by the U.S. Congress. The border question was settled.

THE NEW TERRITORY OF NEW MEXICO

Now living in U.S. territory, the residents of New Mexico soon witnessed extensive changes as the United States consolidated its hold on the northern Rio Grande region. It should be understood that the territory of New Mexico included not only modern-day New Mexico but also included Arizona and the southern portion of Colorado. The portion of the Compromise of 1850, which established New Mexico, was known as the Organic Act of the Territory of New Mexico. By March 1851, a former federal Indian agent, James C. Calhoun, was sworn in as the first governor under the Organic Act. Soon, the first territorial legislative assembly was chosen and seated, Santa Fe was established as the new territorial capital, and New Mexico Territory was divided into three judicial districts.

Soon after, Congress authorized mail routes and post offices in New Mexico. By 1854, U.S. land laws were extended to New Mexico by an act of Congress, and the office of U.S. Surveyor General for the new territory was established. Through the work of this office, the U.S. government established and legitimized Pueblo Indian land claims and recommended the confirmation of 18 pueblo land titles. With a significant Native American presence along the Rio Grande and elsewhere in the region, the U.S. government established military outposts, including Fort Wingate in 1857. And though these official steps encouraged the development of the Rio Grande valley as an area under U.S. control, the transition from Hispanic control was an awkward one.

Although the Treaty of Guadalupe Hidalgo, which ended the Mexican-American War, had promised "the benefits of United States citizenship to Mexican Americans,"[43] as well as the recognition of Spanish and Mexican land grants and their titles, in practice, both matters were commonly ignored by U.S. officials. This proved true in the territory of New Mexico as well as in Texas. Despite the difficulties and tension that sometimes marked relations between the Mexican population of the Rio Grande valley and the Americans, a state of relatively peaceful coexistence evolved. For Native Americans, however, life was harsher.

Since the early days of European colonization of the region, the Native American population had suffered great indignities. While Spain had controlled the Southwest, Spanish authorities had promoted a dual program of subjugation and conversion of the Indians. During the years of Mexican control, Native Americans had gained some autonomy. With the arrival of the Americans and their hands-on approach to governing, however, Native Americans faced new challenges.

One of the immediate effects of the U.S. acquisition of lands in the Southwest was the arrival of thousands of miners whose search for gold and silver disrupted Indian culture patterns and their general way of life. Miners rarely expected to remain for a prolonged period in one place; but although they kept the Native population at arm's length, the presence of so many miners was intrusive. Repeated clashes between miners and Native Americans led to a series of Indian Wars after 1850.

During the early 1860s, U.S. expansion in the territory of New Mexico drove the Apache and Navajo people to fierce resistance. Mescalero Apache and Navajo bands raided mining camps and stole cattle. Utes, Zuñis, and even Mexican-Americans joined in these challenges to the U.S. presence along the Rio Grande valley. U.S. Army Brigadier General James H. Carleton began developing a plan to subjugate the rebellious tribes and contain the resistance. He was not a man known for his patience with the Indians. It became Carleton's mission to round up all renegade Native Americans in the Southwest and place them on a reservation. The site he selected was a dry strip of land between the Rio Grande and the Pecos River. It was called Bosque Redondo, which translates as "circular grove of trees." (For additional information on this Indian reservation, enter "Bosque Redondo" into any search engine and browse the many sites listed.)

Orders to accomplish Carleton's mission were handed to Kit Carson, a mountain man and western guide, then a colonel in the New Mexico Cavalry. Carson launched a difficult but successful campaign against the Mescaleros in 1863. That spring, he brought 400 Mescaleros to Bosque Redondo; another 200 Mescaleros were brought by year's end. For the Mescaleros, the move to the reservation lands was not a dramatic change. Bosque Redondo was near their homelands, and they agreed to move there in exchange for promises of a renewal of peace negotiations. When such talks did not take place, the Mescaleros left the reservation. (Because the Mescaleros probably did not see themselves as having been "captured," they most likely did not view leaving Bosque Redondo as an "escape.")

In the meantime, Carson went after the Navajos. For six grueling months, Carson and his men fought the Navajos in

(continued on page 90)

WAR ON THE RIO GRANDE BORDER

From the beginning of the arrival of the Americans into the region of the Rio Grande, clashes between the Anglos and the Mexican population were common. One clash in the late 1850s escalated into a full-scale revolt.

On a midsummer's day in 1859, Juan Nepomuceno Cortina, a local cattle rancher and lifelong resident of the region, stood on a street in Brownsville, Texas, and watched as a city marshal beat a Mexican worker with the butt of his pistol. Outraged, Cortina demanded the law enforcement official stop the beating. When the marshal refused, Cortina shot him in the shoulder. The Mexican worker and Cortina then rode out of town at a gallop.

Cortina's family had lived in the Lower Rio Grande valley since his great-great-grandfather had entered the then-northern Spanish borderlands during the 1700s. He had seen fellow Mexicans mistreated by local Anglos on many occasions. The scene he witnessed in Brownsville so outraged Cortina that he returned two months later to the Rio Grande town with perhaps as many as 80 followers. Cortina's men broke 12 Mexicans out of the Brownsville jail and killed three Anglos, including the city jailer, whom Cortina accused of having murdered Mexicans. As the raiders raced down Brownsville's streets, they shouted: "Death to the Americans!" and "Viva Mexico." Cortina's raid on Brownsville soon set the stage for a revolt of Mexicans along the Rio Grande.

The self-proclaimed rebel leader soon issued a public proclamation to rally his supporters against the local American population:

> Mexicans! There are . . . [Anglo-American] criminals covered with frightful crimes, but . . . to these monsters indulgence is shown, because they are not of our race. . . . When the State of Texas [became] . . . part of the Union, flocks of vampires, in the guise of men, came and scattered themselves in the settlements. Most of you have been robbed of your property, incarcerated, chased, murdered and hunted like wild beasts. . . . Mexicans! Is there no remedy for you?*

Intent on stopping Cortina, a group of Anglo and Mexican national guardsmen calling themselves the "Brownsville Tigers" raided his ranch but were driven away by Cortina and his men. Unable to catch the elusive Mexican rebel, Anglo authorities began raiding the ranches of neighboring Mexican-Americans. Later, a group of Texas Rangers was dispatched to capture Cortina. They engaged the Mexican leader's men, but Cortina sent the Rangers scattering.

During the months that followed, Cortina became a heroic figure in the eyes of many local Mexicans. The rebel leader rampaged along the Lower Rio Grande valley, receiving support, shelter, and food from "sympathetic Mexicans on both sides of the border."[**] His reputation spread up and down the Rio Grande, and he became known as the "Robin Hood of the Rio Grande." A Mexican newspaper in San Antonio ran alarming headlines about Cortina and his regional revolution:

> THE MEXICAN POPULACE ARMING TO EXTERMINATE THE AMERICANS AND RECONQUER OUR COUNTRY TO THE COLORADO RIVER! ACTUAL WAR ON THE BORDER!

After seemingly endless weeks of spreading violence, bloodshed, and fear, Cortina was finally cornered in Rio Grande City, 100 miles upriver from Brownsville, where he and his men had engaged in a shootout with Texas Rangers and U.S. Army troops. Miraculously, Cortina managed to escape, but not before "he faced his pursuers, emptied his revolver, and tried to halt his panic-stricken men."[***]

Driven out of the eastern Rio Grande valley, Cortina established a base in Mexico where he remained for the next 15 years, raiding across the Rio Grande and stealing cattle from Anglo ranches. He was finally captured in 1875 and ordered by the Mexican government to Mexico City, far away from the valley of the Rio Grande where his cause and reputation had managed to excite borderland Mexicans for nearly a generation.

  [*] Ward, 179–180.
 [**] Ibid., 180.
[***] Ibid., 182.

Kit Carson was appointed U.S. Indian agent for northern New Mexico in 1853, and after the Navajos refused to be confined to a reservation, he began a barbarous economic war against the tribe in 1863, destroying their crops, livestock, and orchards. By 1864, most Navajos had surrendered to Carson and they were led on the infamous "Long Walk," a 300-mile-long trek from Arizona to Fort Sumner, New Mexico—the location of Bosque Redondo Reservation.

(continued from page 87)

the harsh, rugged backcountry of the Rio Grande valley. Although Carson was often unable to track down and fight directly with Navajo warriors, he burned their homes and fields, "rounded up their sheep, hacked down their peach orchards."[44] Through this "scorched-earth" policy, Carson slowly wore down Navajo resistance. By the winter of 1864, the Navajos, driven to the point of starvation, were surrendering to the U.S. Army by the hundreds. Thousands of Navajos, however, remained at large, holding out for two more years before surrendering. When they finally turned themselves in, Carson ordered 8,500 Navajo men, women, and children to march 350 miles to eastern New Mexico. The march, known today as the "Long Walk," proved deadly. Carson had not prepared for the massive numbers of Navajos he had to escort to Bosque Redondo. Food and blankets were in short supply, and hundreds of Navajos died along the route. Moreover, "Ute and New Mexicans shadowing the slow-moving columns seized stragglers and sold them as slaves."[45] Those who finally reached the reservation designated for them by General Carleton suffered even greater difficulties:

> There was no game, not enough fertile land for farming, too little grass even for goats. The meager crops that did grow fell victim to cutworms and sudden downpours. Thin government clothing kept no one warm in winter. Bickering between the army and the Indian bureau meant supplies often arrived late, or not at all. . . . Carleton insisted that the Navajo live in adobe houses, but they refused . . . since their religion forbade them to continue to live in a structure in which someone had died— and they were dying fast.[46]

For four years, the Navajos remained within the confines of Bosque Redondo, a period in their history they came to refer to as *Nahonzod*, the "Time of Fear." Then, in 1868, in a complete turnaround in policy, they were allowed to return to their homelands. By that time, however, one in four Navajos had already died.

THE COMING OF THE RAILROADS

As the Native populations of the Rio Grande were subdued during the 1860s, 1870s, and 1880s, the region witnessed extraordinary change and economic development. A significant portion of the development of the Rio Grande region hinged on the arrival of an essential and rapidly developing transportation system in nineteenth-century America—railroads. The first rail system to link the eastern United States and the West Coast of California was completed in 1869 with the uniting of tracks at Promontory Point, Utah. This joint construction of two railway companies, the Union Pacific and the Central Pacific, laid the groundwork for the building of other rail systems across the American West, including in the Rio Grande region.

Within a decade, the Southern Pacific Railroad had laid track out of California across the Southwest to Tucson, Arizona. By 1880, the line reached the Rio Grande community of El Paso, which by then had 10,000 residents. The Southern Pacific Line was not the first to reach New Mexico and the Rio Grande. Another rail system had entered New Mexico just a few years earlier. During the mid-1860s a railroad entrepreneur, Cyrus K. Holliday, set out to build a line between two Kansas towns—Topeka and Atchison. Although the Civil War delayed the construction of his intended short rail line, once construction began, he decided to extend his railway to link the Kansas towns with the old Santa Fe Trail and towns in the Southwest. The railroad would be known as the Atchison, Topeka, & Santa Fe.

Construction on the line between Atchison and Topeka began in 1868 and was completed by the spring of the following year. Another decade would pass before the Santa Fe leg of the railway crossed the border into New Mexico. By then, other railroads were challenging the Santa Fe line. One of these, the Denver & Rio Grande Railroad was incorporated in October

1870, and labor crews began laying rails the following summer. The plan was for the railway to begin in Denver, extend south to Santa Fe and on to El Paso, and eventually end up with a terminal in Mexico City. By October 1871, the line had reached Colorado Springs, but then construction efforts were slowed by financial problems. Five years later, the Denver & Rio Grande had reached the Rio Grande valley and stood at the southern border of Colorado, poised to move through the only possible border gap in the southern Rockies leading into northern New Mexico—Raton Pass. Some deft maneuvering by the Atchison, Topeka, & Santa Fe allowed the Denver & Rio Grande's rival to establish itself in the pass first.

By the autumn of 1878, construction had begun on the Santa Fe line through Raton Pass. By July 1, 1879, the Atchison, Topeka, & Santa Fe Railroad had reached Las Vegas, New Mexico, and just three days later, a train reached a "makeshift depot at the former Mexican port of entry on the Santa Fe Trail."[47] The people of Santa Fe were unhappy that the railroad's engineers and planners had selected a route that ran on the opposite side of the Santa Fe River, a tributary of the Rio Grande, missing Santa Fe's plaza by over a mile. Over time, however, the original Santa Fe, known as "Old Town," had spread across the river, and one of America's oldest continually occupied communities reached a new milestone in its progress: The first train to reach Old Santa Fe finally arrived in February 1880.

Despite the success of the Atchison, Topeka & Santa Fe in reaching the Rio Grande valley ahead of the Denver & Rio Grande, the Denver & Rio Grande did continue on to the farthest northern reaches of the river in southern Colorado where it served mining towns such as Leadville. Other railroad companies also reached the Rio Grande valley during the 1880s. The Missouri Pacific built a line from St. Louis and New Orleans to the West, connecting with Texas Gulf towns.

(continued on page 96)

THE RAILROAD RIVALS RACE TO RATON

Following the successful completion of the first transcontinental railroad from Omaha, Nebraska, to Sacramento, California, a furious age of railroad construction began, one that lasted for nearly half a century. During the 1870s, railroad companies competed for access to the best routes. One such competition developed between the Santa Fe Railroad and the Denver & Rio Grande Railroad along the Colorado–New Mexico border of the Upper Rio Grande. At the center of the rivalry stood an odd, former mountain man named Richard Lacy Wootton, a man known to friends and acquaintances in the southern Rockies as "Uncle Dick."

Richard Wootton was a western legend even before he became a part of the rivalry for routes between competing railroads. Weighing "two hundred hard-muscled pounds, with a wild shock of bristling black hair to match,"* Wootton had trapped beaver, hunted with Kit Carson, fought Indians, killed grizzly bears, served as a scout in the Mexican War, worked as a freighter on the Santa Fe Trail, and operated a stagecoach line out of Missouri.

By the time he was 50, he had little to show for his years of work. In 1866, in an effort to provide financial security for his later years, Wootton bought 2,500 acres of New Mexico–Colorado borderland surrounding Raton Pass and received permission from state officials in both territories to establish a toll road through the pass. He then set to work "blasting boulders, felling trees, bridging and grading the twenty-seven-mile route"** through the lower Sangre de Cristo Mountains. With the commonly used pass under his management, Wootton began charging $1.50 per wagon, a quarter per horse and rider, and five cents for each head of cattle or sheep. Raton Pass became Wootton's ticket to a prosperous future. In one 15-month period, the tolls collected added up to nearly $10,000.

By the mid-1870s, regional western railroads began eyeing Raton Pass as the only viable route for a rail line crossing the New Mexico–Colorado border. During 1876, field crews for the Denver & Rio Grande Railroad began surveying the pass, intent on getting permission from Wootton to use it for their rail line into New Mexico. As Denver & Rio Grande crews surveyed Raton Pass, a rival engineer, Raymond Morley, was also moving through the pass, posing as a shepherd. Morley, moreover, was an engineer for the Atchison, Topeka & Santa Fe line, which had already initiated discussions about the pass with Wootton.

Soon each company was scrambling to gain the rights to a railroad through the pass ahead of the competition. In February 1878, the Santa Fe sent three construction engineers, including Morley, to begin construction on a line through the pass ahead of the Denver & Rio Grande. Officials at the Denver & Rio Grande were aware of their rival's intentions, having intercepted the telegrams the general manager of the Santa Fe had sent to Morley and his colleagues in Pueblo, where the two railroad companies shared a telegraph line.

The race was on. The Santa Fe engineers took a Denver & Rio Grande train headed to the rail town closest to Raton Pass. While onboard, they spotted a pair of Denver & Rio Grande chief engineers, also headed to Raton Pass. Desperate to reach the pass ahead of their rivals, Morley and one of his associates jumped the train at El Moro and hired a buggy, "dashing through the freezing February night to the tollhouse at the foot of the pass."*** Once there, they awoke Wootton and explained their intentions. Luckily for the Santa Fe engineers, the old retired mountain man had no love for the Denver & Rio Grande since the rival railroad company had a habit of establishing its own towns along its rail lines, controlling trade along those towns, and thus putting preexisting towns out of business. Wootton agreed to cooperate with Morley. Desperate to ensure Wootton's continued cooperation, the Santa Fe engineers offered him $50,000 for his toll road. Oddly, Wootton turned down their offer, settling instead for a free lifetime pass on the Santa Fe and $25 a month for groceries. What happened next soon became the stuff of railroad legend:

> "Sure I'll help," Wootton told Morley. . . . Back into the house he went, collared some freighters and Trinidad youngsters who were having a dance, handed them shovels, and hurried them out into the darkness. When the Denver and Rio Grande's crew puffed up the trail half an hour later, they stared in dismay at an odd assortment of graders shoveling like beaver under the light of Wootton's lanterns. Raton Pass belonged to the Santa Fe by right of prior possession.[+]

Having gained the upper hand over the Denver & Rio Grande, the Santa Fe line was prepared to build the first rail line through Raton Pass. By the fall of 1878, tracks were laid past Wootton's toll station and on December 1, a train crossed from Colorado into New Mexico. When the rail line was finally completed, the first locomotive to reach northern New Mexico from southern Colorado was named after the local western legend who had helped make it possible—"Uncle Dick."

* David Lavender, *The Big Divide: The Lively Story of the People of the Southern Rocky Mountains from Yellowstone to Santa Fe* (Edison, N.J.: Castle Books, 2001), 155.
** Ibid., 156.
*** Ibid., 157.
+ Ibid.

(continued from page 93)

The Texas & Pacific reached Laredo on the Rio Grande, and the line later became part of the Southern Pacific Railroad. Another line, the Galveston, Harrisburg, & San Antonio arrived in El Paso in 1880. By 1881, the tracks of the Santa Fe reached Albuquerque and joined with the Southern Pacific that spring at Deming, New Mexico. With the joining of the Santa Fe and the Southern Pacific, the residents of the Rio Grande valley were connected to markets as far away as Kansas City.

Throughout the final decades of the nineteenth century, the changes brought to the Rio Grande valley by the arrival of the railroads were extensive: The railroads influenced the development of farming, mining, the cattle industry, and other major contributors to the economy of the Southwest. In New Mexico, some of the early mines were restored to new productivity, and a number of new mines were opened during the 1880s and 1890s. The railroads delivered heavy equipment for the processing and extraction of greater amounts of metal, including silver, gold, and copper. The ores mined in the region were processed and shipped out by the same rail systems that had brought in the mining equipment.

The development of mining and other industries in the Rio Grande valley encouraged a new phase of immigration into the region. In 1870, the non-Indian population of New Mexico had reached 100,000. Within 30 years, that number doubled to 200,000. Adding the Native American population, the number of people in New Mexico stood just short of 400,000. By 1912, New Mexico, after more than 60 years as a United States territory, became the nation's forty-seventh state. The Rio Grande now flowed through three American states.

8

A River in
Constant Demand

Throughout the twentieth century, the waters of the Rio Grande have been the subject of constant and recurring water reclamation projects. As more people moved into the Rio Grande valley, larger and larger population centers developed, creating a greater need for economic expansion and water management, most of which took the form of irrigation projects. Irrigation water diverted from the Rio Grande was nothing new. Native Americans in the Southwest had diverted the river's waters, as had the Spanish colonists and Mexican inhabitants. Even during the years between 1850 and 1900, the Native American population along the river irrigated approximately 20,000 acres. The region supported increasing populations during those decades, and overall irrigation of the Rio Grande valley reached 125,000 acres by 1880. These irrigation projects suffered dramatically when the Rio Grande experienced repeated flooding during the latter decades of the nineteenth century and the early decades of the twentieth century. In the region surrounding Albuquerque, including the Sandia Canyons, there were major floods in 1874, 1884, 1891, 1903, 1909, 1912, and 1920. The 1874 flood left 24 square miles of desert land around Albuquerque inundated for about three months.

One early-twentieth-century effort to develop large-scale irrigation on the middle portion of the Rio Grande basin took place in 1909 with the building of a pumping station operated by the Louisiana–Rio Grande Canal Company. The company's river system rerouted water to thousands of acres of West Texas farmland, some as far as ten miles from the river. Hidalgo, Texas, situated along the lower reaches of the Rio Grande not far from the Gulf Coast, constructed its own large pumping facility "complete with boilers, sixty-inch pumps, engines, and a large smokestack to supply irrigation to forty thousand acres of thirsty crops."[48]

The U.S. government played a significant role in encouraging the development of the Rio Grande's water resources with the

Completed in 1916, Elephant Butte Dam, four miles east of Truth or Consequences, New Mexico, is the largest dam on the Rio Grande. The dam's reservoir covers approximately 180 square miles and is used for flood control, hydroelectric power, and irrigation.

passage, in 1902, of a reclamation act authorizing the sale of federal bonds to pay for the construction of dams, reservoirs, and other water-management facilities. Such programs became common along the Rio Grande and other rivers in the Southwest over the subsequent decades. Similar projects were soon underway along the Pecos River in New Mexico and the Salt River in Arizona. The Elephant Butte Dam at Hot Springs, a New Mexico community known today as Truth or Consequences, was completed in 1916 and included more than 360 miles of irrigation canals spreading across south-central New Mexico. The waters held back by the dam created a storage lake with a volume of 1.3 million acre-feet of water.

THE JOINING OF THE SOUTHWEST'S TWO GREAT RIVERS

Whereas the Rio Grande flows out of the southern Rockies as one of the Southwest's most important rivers, another significant waterway emerges from the Rockies and crosses the desert lands of the Southwest—the Colorado. Although the Colorado flows west, away from the waters of the Rio Grande, the two rivers were joined together by a man-made diversion system in the 1960s.

During the 1930s, the construction of the Elephant Butte Dam was designed to provide a vast water reservoir for New Mexico and Texas communities farther downstream. The dam did nothing for the upriver communities, including New Mexico's largest city, Albuquerque. As the city grew in population, it needed more water than the Rio Grande could provide. In the 1960s, the U.S. Congress authorized a different kind of water project to help deliver water to Albuquerque and other upriver towns.

Called the San Juan–Chama Project (SJCP), the plan called for the excavation of a canal and three immense tunnels to be bored through the Rocky Mountains and filled with water diverted from the Upper San Juan River, a tributary of the Colorado. The tunnels were to deliver water into the natural course of the Chama River, which would reach the Rio Grande.

The entire project presented a herculean challenge to hydroengineering. The canal was an enormous challenge in its own right. In addition, 26 miles of tunnels were carved beneath the Continental Divide. Giant mechanical "moles" were used to burrow out the huge tunnels. When brought "on line," these delivery tunnels were capable of diverting water at the rate of 650 cubic yards per second. With the opening of the completed project in 1968, the San Juan–Chama Diversion Project was able to deliver nearly 100,000 acre-feet of water to the Upper Rio Grande, a boon to a region of the river experiencing rapid and sustained growth.

Irrigation enabled the area to be farmed and thus the Rio Grande, from its upper reaches to its lower course, witnessed an expansion of agriculture. In West Texas, farmers and ranchers began developing the High Plains region, relying on irrigation, "especially in the lower Rio Grande valley."[49] This farming area saw significant development with the arrival of the St. Louis, Brownsville & Mexico Railroad, which had laid tracks and was in operation by 1904. The railroad allowed the shipment of citrus fruits and vegetables, raised under irrigation, without spoilage. By 1914, commercial orchards were in operation and fruit growers determined that "grafted grapefruit and oranges on the native orange stock would produce a tree adapted to the Rio Grande soil and climate." [50] Between 1920 and 1930, as irrigation and farming expanded, the population along the Lower Rio Grande valley doubled.

By the 1930s, another dam was constructed on the Rio Grande, the Caballo facility, just 17 miles downriver from the Elephant Butte Dam. With an expanded capacity for irrigation, agriculture along the Rio Grande valley developed at an accelerated pace. The deserts of southern New Mexico began to produce abundant harvests. Approximately three of every four acres under irrigated cultivation produced cotton, various hays, and pecans; the remaining acres produced a mix of vegetables, corn, chili peppers, and onions.

With so much irrigation taking place in the United States, the issue of water in the Southwest and the fair use of the Rio Grande led to a conference between the United States and Mexico, which share an extensive border delineated by the Rio Grande. In 1933, the conference resulted in the Rio Grande Rectification treaty between the two countries, which straightened out the river east of El Paso.

A similar agreement was reached five years later between the states of Colorado, New Mexico, and Texas, which the Rio Grande flows through. This document, known as the Rio Grande Compact, determined water distribution for that portion of the river not already allocated to Mexico. Both the Rio Grande Compact and the Rio Grande Rectification treaty helped encourage a dramatic expansion of acreage of the Southwest under irrigation along the middle and lower courses of the river. By the 1950s, the treaty with Mexico had led to the construction of a large water management project, the International Falcon Dam, which is situated on the Rio Grande, just east of Laredo, Texas.

Throughout the twentieth century, irrigation projects continued to expand as populations in the deserts of New Mexico and Texas as well as the mountain communities of southern Colorado continued to grow. By the 1990s, New Mexico alone was supporting at least 1 million acres of irrigated land, the centerpiece of the state's economy. The Rio Grande also supplied water for an additional 1 million acres in West Texas, much of that land being used for citrus tree cultivation. A 1993 study of the use of the Rio Grande determined that nearly 90 percent "of the Rio Grande River basin's water resources are devoted exclusively to irrigation."[51]

Over the past century and a half, industry has also helped develop the economic base of the Rio Grande region. In Colorado, mines still dot the landscape near the source waters of the river, and "enormous quantities of water are used in an extraction process for gold and silver called flotation milling."[52] Farther south, the river is flanked by chemical plants, food processing facilities, and textile factories. In Texas, cotton produced in irrigated fields is loaded onto trucks and delivered to local textile mills situated near the Rio Grande. Millions of gallons of water are drawn from the river to clean the raw cotton. Once the cotton is spun and woven onto huge bolts, more water is needed to fill giant dye vats. After it is dyed, the newly spun cotton cloth is again washed with water. Each step utilized in processing locally grown cotton requires water from the Rio Grande system.

The grand old river of the Southwest also continues to support sprawling urban populations. Throughout the twentieth century, small towns established during the nineteenth century and earlier developed into large metropolitan areas. During the 1990s, the fastest population growth in Texas was centered in three areas: Austin, the suburbs of Houston, and the cities along the Rio Grande in Southwest Texas (from El Paso to Brownsville).

The numbers tell the story of urban development along the Rio Grande during the twentieth century. Between 1880 and 2000, the population of El Paso grew from 10,000 to 650,000. The wild nineteenth-century border town of Laredo was home to fewer than 4,000 during the 1880s. By the end of the twentieth century, Laredo's population had surpassed 200,000. Albuquerque experienced sustained and dramatic growth during those same years. At the beginning of the Civil War, fewer than 2,000 people lived in the new territorial capital. By the turn of the century, 8,000 lived there and, 20 years later, with the expansion of irrigated farmlands, the population of Albuquerque had grown to 15,000. By 1950, nearly 100,000 called Albuquerque home, and the population reached a quarter million by 1970. Today, Albuquerque provides water to support 450,000 citizens; much of which is drawn from the Rio Grande. With such constant population increases, not only in New Mexico and Texas but in Mexico, the strain on the water resources of the Southwest in general and on the watershed of the Rio Grande in particular has reached critical mass.

Urban centers, both in the United States and Mexico, tap incredible quantities of water from the Rio Grande. Today, El Paso and Albuquerque draw approximately 18 billion gallons annually from the Rio Grande's water system. As these and other Rio Grande communities have exploded in growth since the mid-twentieth century, additional major dam systems have been constructed to facilitate water management, including the facility at Falcon, Texas (completed in 1954); another at Del Rio, Texas (1969); and a third at Cochiti, New Mexico (1975).

By 1993, an important U.S. river conservation organization, American Rivers, declared the Rio Grande and the Rio Conchos to be the most endangered river systems in the United States.

The environmental organization expressed concerns about the declining quality of the rivers' water. Pollutants from mining along the Upper Rio Grande as well as from factory and city wastes had been allowed to seep into the river from both Mexican and U.S. border towns and cities. Massive farming all along the river had threatened the Rio Grande system with intolerable levels of pesticides and fertilizers. Some of these problems persist even today.

Water diversion is a growing and alarming problem along the Rio Grande. Although the reservoirs at dams such as Elephant Butte and Caballo are able to release approximately 800,000 acre-feet of water each year, the flow is tapped so significantly for irrigation and municipal use that "by the time the Rio Grande reaches the city of Presidio, Texas, just north of its confluence with the Conchos River, it is entirely depleted."[53] Between El Paso and Presidio, the Rio Grande is often a dry riverbed. Only with the flow of water from Mexico's Conchos River and other downstream tributaries has the Rio Grande been revitalized; its course reestablished to flow farther south toward, but not always to, the Gulf of Mexico.

As early as 1945, the Rio Grande failed to reach the Gulf of Mexico, its waters simply petering out in the marshy delta lands near its mouth. From 1945 on, the river has stopped short of the Gulf at an increasing rate. Since 1990, the Rio Grande has run out of water before reaching the Gulf nearly a dozen years.

Despite these ecological limitations on the Rio Grande and its tributary systems, the river remains a vital source of recreation for countless millions. The reservoirs adjacent to the river's dams provide opportunities for fishing, swimming, boating, water skiing and jet skiing, and scuba diving. Elephant Butte Lake is among the river's most popular sporting and camping spots. The lake, covering approximately 180 square miles, is the Rio Grande's largest and stretches back from its holding dam to a distance of 45 miles. In places, it is four miles wide. The lake

As recently as 1993, the Rio Grande had been declared the most endangered river system in the United States. However, environmental organizations such as American Rivers have endeavored to return the Rio Grande to its natural state. If all goes well, projects such as the release of the silvery minnow (shown here) will be a step toward returning the river to its natural environment.

provides multiple advantages for those who enjoy the outdoors. Tourists, vacationers, water enthusiasts, and sportsmen pump $200 million annually into the economy based along the waters of the Rio Grande valley.

With each passing year of the twenty-first century, river experts and hydrologists can only speculate whether the Rio Grande will continue to flow along its historical course from its Rocky Mountain headwaters to the Gulf of Mexico. The future of the Rio Grande remains a matter of speculation. How much longer this great working river of the Southwest, one whose waters are tapped repeatedly along its 1,900-mile-long course, can sustain itself is a question only time will answer.

20000 B.C. Modern archaeological excavations suggest this date for earliest human occupation of the Rio Grande valley.

A.D. 1200 Ancient Anasazi peoples begin to abandon their pueblo villages and cliff dwellings along the Rio Grande.

1300–1500 Modern Native American tribes of the Southwest have evolved.

1519 Spanish fleet captain, Alonso Alvarez de Pineda's ships reach the mouth of the Rio Grande; the expedition fails to establish a colony on the river.

1523 Spanish Governor Francisco Garay reaches the river's mouth to establish a colony but fails in his attempt.

1525 King Charles V establishes the Rio Grande as the western boundary of Spanish provincial Florida.

20000 B.C.
Humans begin to settle the Rio Grande valley

A.D. 1200
Anasazi begin to abandon their cliff dwellings

1680
Pueblo Revolt led by Pope; several hundred Spanish killed

1610
Santa Fe becomes provincial capital of Spanish New Mexico

20000 B.C.   **A.D. 1200**   **1600**   **1800**

1525
Rio Grande set as western boundary of Spanish provincial Florida by King Charles V

1790s
Spanish establish parish churches in Santa Fe, Albuquerque, and El Paso

1540–1541
Coronado reaches the Rio Grande

1598
Don Juan de Oñate establishes the first permanent Spanish colony on the Rio Grande

1528–1536 Cabeza de Vaca wanders along the Rio Grande valley with other survivors of Spanish shipwreck.

1540–1541 Spanish conquistador Francisco de Coronado reaches the Rio Grande during overland exploration campaign.

1581–1593 Four Spanish expeditions reach the waters of the Rio Grande; all fail to establish a permanent Spanish colony in the region.

1598 Spanish leader Don Juan de Oñate attempts to establish a Rio Grande colony; his efforts yield a permanent colony.

1610 Oñate's replacement as governor, Don Pedro de Peralta, establishes Santa Fe as the capital of the Spanish colony of New Mexico in the Rio Grande valley.

1821
Mexican Republic established after revolt against Spain

1912
New Mexico becomes the forty-seventh state

1920–1930
Population along the Lower Rio Grande valley doubles during this decade

1876
Denver & Rio Grande Railroad reaches the Upper Rio Grande valley

1950s
International Falcon Dam constructed near Laredo, Texas

1825   **1900**   **2000**

1846–1848
Mexican–American War; U.S. gains undisputed control of Texas, and what would later become California, New Mexico, and Arizona

1990s
Ninety percent of Rio Grande water is devoted to irrigation

1845
United States annexes Texas from Mexico; Texas becomes the twenty-eighth state to enter the Union

1933
United States and Mexico sign Rio Grande Rectification treaty that determines water distribution for the Rio Grande

1680   Pueblo Revolt in New Mexico results in the evacuation and burning of Santa Fe; the revolt represents a serious setback for Spanish power in the Upper Rio Grande region.

1692–1696   Spanish carry out major military campaign into New Mexico to regain control of the region of the Rio Grande and recapture Santa Fe.

1790s   Spanish parish churches are established in the Rio Grande towns of Santa Fe, Albuquerque, Santa Cruz de la Canada, and El Paso.

1821   Successful, conservative revolution in Mexico results in the removal of Spanish power in New Spain and the establishment of a Mexican Republic controlled by the Mexican people.

1820s   Mexicans and Americans establish trade connections along the Santa Fe Trail into the Rio Grande valley.

1820–30s   American fur trappers and mountain men enter Mexican-controlled Santa Fe from the north.

1832   Two Texas statehood conventions claim the Rio Grande as the one true border of West Texas.

1836   Texan revolutionaries defeat Mexican President Santa Anna who signs a peace treaty recognizing the Rio Grande as the border between Texas and Mexico.

1840s   U.S. government annexes Texas as a new state, fomenting a war between Mexico and the United States; the United States claims the Rio Grande as the southwestern border of the new state of Texas.

1846–1848   War erupts between the United States and Mexico and fighting takes place along the banks of the Rio Grande; U.S. military commander, Stephen Kearny captures Santa Fe; the war ends with the annexation of Mexico's northern borderlands, including California, Arizona, and New Mexico; the Treaty of Guadalupe Hidalgo establishes the Rio Grande as Texas' western border.

1848 Citizens of Santa Fe hold a convention and adopt petitions calling for New Mexico to be granted territorial status by the U.S. government.

1854 U.S. land laws are extended to New Mexico and Rio Grande valley.

1860s U.S. expansion into the territory of New Mexico leads the Apache and Navajo people to fierce resistance.

1863–1864 U.S. Colonel Kit Carson, former mountain man and western guide, launches a campaign to subdue the Mescalero Apaches and the Navajos and place them on a reservation at Bosque Redondo, located between the Rio Grande and the Pecos River.

1874 Flooding along the Rio Grande results in serious damage in Albuquerque.

1876 Denver & Rio Grande Railroad reaches the Upper Rio Grande valley of southern Colorado.

1879 Atchison, Topeka, & Santa Fe Railroad reaches Santa Fe.

1880 Rail line reaches the Rio Grande town of El Paso; 125,000 acres of land along the Rio Grande valley are irrigated.

1909 Louisiana–Rio Grande Canal Company opens pumping station on the Rio Grande and delivers water to thousands of acres of farmland.

1912   New Mexico becomes the forty-seventh state.

1916   Elephant Butte Dam project is completed; more than 360 miles of irrigation canals spread across south-central New Mexico.

1920–1930   Population along the Lower Rio Grande valley doubles in a decade.

1933   Rio Grande Rectification treaty between the United States and Mexico delineates water distribution along the Rio Grande; construction on the dam at Caballo begins.

1938   Meeting of representatives from Colorado, New Mexico, and Texas results in Rio Grande Compact, which determines water distribution of Rio Grande water not allocated for Mexico.

1950s   International Falcon Dam is constructed on the Rio Grande, just upriver from Laredo, Texas.

1968   The San Juan–Chama Diversion Project begins delivering water from the Upper San Juan to the Rio Grande.

1990s   Ninety percent of the Rio Grande water resources are devoted to irrigation; for several years, the Rio Grande fails to reach the Gulf of Mexico.

1993   Conservation organization American Rivers declares the Rio Grande to be one of the United States' most endangered rivers.

CHAPTER 1:
Ancient River; Ancient People

1 Paul Horgan, *Great River: The Rio Grande in North American History*, vol. 1. (New York: Rinehart & Company, 1954), 6.

2 *http://www.unm.edu/~abqteach/ EnvirCUs/99-03-04.htm.*

3 James Barter, *Rivers of the World: The Rio Grande* (San Diego, Calif.: Lucent Books, 2003), 24.

CHAPTER 2:
Tribes along the Rio Grande

4 Alvin M. Josephy, Jr., *The Indian Heritage of America* (Boston, Mass.: Houghton Mifflin, 1991), 162.

5 New Mexico State Engineer Office, "Acequias," July 1997: *http://www.century21 landsun.com/Ranches/Acequias.html.*

6 Ibid.

7 David Roberts, *In Search of the Old Ones: Exploring the Anasazi World of the Southwest* (New York: Simon & Schuster, 1997), 38.

CHAPTER 3:
The Spanish Arrive

8 Horgan, vol. 1, 86.

9 Ibid.

10 Ibid., 94.

11 Graham Raht, *The Romance of Davis Mountains and Big Bend Country: A History* (Odessa, Tex.: The Rahtbooks Company, 1963), 9.

12 Ibid.

CHAPTER 4:
Colonizing the Rio Grande

13 Horgan, vol. 1, 154.

14 Raht, 29.

15 Lynn Perrigo, *The American Southwest: Its People and Cultures* (Albuquerque, N.M.: University of New Mexico Press, 1975), 30.

16 Ibid.

17 Ibid., 33.

18 Ibid.

19 George P. Hammond and Agipito Rey, eds., *Don Juan de Onate: Colonizer of New Mexico* (Albuquerque, N.M.: University of New Mexico Press, 1953), 248.

20 Perrigo, 41.

21 *The Spanish West* (Alexandria, Va.: Time-Life Books, 1976), 51.

22 Ibid., 52.

23 Ibid.

24 Ibid.

CHAPTER 5:
Mexicans and Americans

25 Geoffrey Ward, *The West: An Illustrated History* (Boston, Mass.: Little, Brown and Company, 1996), 28.

26 Time-Life, 131.

27 Horgan, vol. 2, 496.

28 Ibid., 497.

29 Time-Life, 142.

30 Ibid.

CHAPTER 6:
A War over the Rio Grande

31 Carol and Thomas Christensen, *The U.S.–Mexican War* (San Francisco, Calif.: Bay Books, 1998), 57.

32 Ibid., 58.

33 Ibid., 69.

34 Ibid., 109.

35 Perrigo, 156.

36 Christensen, 110.

37 Ibid., 112.

38 Ibid., 113.

CHAPTER 7:
The Americans Arrive

39 Rupert N. Richardson, et al., *Texas: The Lone Star State* (Upper Saddle River, N.J.: Prentice Hall, 2001), 162.

40 Perrigo, 164.

41 Richardson, 164.

42 Ibid., 165.

43 Ward, 179.

44 Ibid., 198.

45 Ibid.

46 Ibid.

47 Perrigo, 292.

CHAPTER 8:
A River in Constant Demand

48 Barter, 47.

49 Richardson, 304.

50 Ibid.

51 Sherman R. Ellis, et al., "Rio Grande Valley, Colorado, New Mexico, and Texas," *American Water Resources Association Bulletin*, vol. 29, no. 4, 1993, 619.

52 Barter, 52.

53 Ibid., 60.

Athearn, Robert G. *The Denver and Rio Grande Western Railroad: Rebel of the Rockies.* Lincoln, Nebr.: University of Nebraska Press, 1962.

Bancroft, Hubert Howe. *History of Arizona and New Mexico, 1530–1888.* Albuquerque, N.M.: Horn & Wallace Publishers, 1962.

Barter, James. *Rivers of the World: The Rio Grande.* San Diego, Calif.: Lucent Books, 2003.

Bauer, Karl Jack. *The Mexican War, 1846–1848.* New York: Macmillan, 1974.

Christensen, Carol and Thomas. *The U.S.–Mexican War.* San Francisco, Calif.: Bay Books, 1998.

Danneman, Mike. *Rio Grande through the Rockies.* Waukesha, Wisc.: Kalmbach, 2002.

Driggs, Howard R. *Rise of the Lone Star: A Story of Texas Told by Its Pioneers.* New York: Frederick A. Stokes Company, 1936.

Edwards, Frank S. *A Campaign in New Mexico.* Ann Arbor, Mich.: University Microfilms, 1966.

Ellis, Sherman R., Gary W. Levings, Lisa F. Carter, Steven F. Richey, and Mary Jo Rodell. "Rio Grande Valley, Colorado, New Mexico, and Texas," *American Water Resources Association Bulletin.* Vol. 29, No. 4, 1993.

Fahey, Kathleen. *The Rio Grande.* Milwaukee, Wisc.: Gareth Stevens Publishing, 2004.

Fehrenbach, T.R. *Lone Star: A History of Texas and the Texans.* New York: Macmillan, 1968.

Griffin-Pierce, Trudy. *The Encyclopedia of Native America.* New York: Viking, 1995.

Hammond, George P., and Agipito Rey, eds. *Don Juan de Onate: Colonizer of New Mexico.* Albuquerque, N.M.: University of New Mexico Press, 1953.

Hollon, W. Eugene. *The Southwest: Old and New.* Lincoln, Nebr.: University of Nebraska Press, 1961.

Horgan, Paul. *Great River: The Rio Grande in North American History.* Vols. 1–2. New York: Rinehart & Company, 1954.

Inman, Henry. *The Old Santa Fe Trail: The Story of a Great Highway.* Williamstown, Mass.: Corner House Publishers, 1977.

Johannsen, Robert W. *To the Halls of the Montezumas: The Mexican War in the American Imagination.* New York: Oxford University Press, 1985.

Josephy, Alvin M. *The Indian Heritage of America.* Boston, Mass.: Houghton Mifflin, 1991.

Lavender, David. *The Big Divide: The Lively Story of the People of the Southern Rocky Mountains from Yellowstone to Santa Fe.* Edison, N.J.: Castle Books, 2001.

Lourie, Peter. *Rio Grande: From the Rocky Mountains to the Gulf of Mexico.* Honesdale, Pa.: Boyds Mills Press, 1999.

McWilliams, Carey. *North from Mexico: The Spanish-Speaking People of the United States.* Philadelphia, Pa.: J.B. Lippincott Company, 1949.

Perrigo, Lynn. *The American Southwest: Its People and Cultures.* Albuquerque, N.M.: University of New Mexico Press, 1975.

Raht, Carlysle Graham. *The Romance of Davis Mountains and Big Bend Country: A History.* Odessa, Tex.: The Rahtbooks Company, 1963.

Richardson, Rupert, Adrian Anderson, Cary D. Wintz, and Ernest Wallace. *Texas: The Lone Star State.* Upper Saddle River, N.J.: Prentice Hall, 2001.

Roberts, David. *In Search of the Old Ones: Exploring the Anasazi World of the Southwest.* New York: Simon & Schuster, 1997.

The Spanish West. Alexandria, Va.: Time-Life Books, 1976.

Tesar, Jenny. *America's Top 10 Rivers.* Woodbridge, Conn.: Blackbirch Press, 1998.

Ward, Geoffrey. *The West: An Illustrated History.* Boston, Mass.: Little, Brown and Company, 1996.

Weisman, Alan. *La Frontera: The United States Border with Mexico.* San Diego, Calif.: Harcourt Brace Jovanovich, 1986.

Wishart, David J. *The Fur Trade of the American West, 1807–1840.* Lincoln, Nebr.: University of Nebraska Press, 1992.

Workers of the Writers' Program of the Work Projects Administration in the State of New Mexico. *New Mexico: A Guide to the Colorful State.* New York: Hastings House Publishers, 1940.

Folsom, Franklin. *Indian Uprising on the Rio Grande: The Pueblo Revolt of 1680.* Albuquerque, N.M.: University of New Mexico Press, 1996.

Gibson, Daniel. *Pueblos of the Rio Grande.* Tucson, Ariz.: Rio Nuevo Publishers, 2002.

Griffin, James. *Rio Grande Railroad.* St. Paul, Minn.: Motorbooks International, 2003.

Havenhill, Jackye. *Texas Legends.* Unionville, N.Y.: Royal Fireworks Press, 1997.

Horgan, Paul. *Great River: The Rio Grande in North American History.* Vols. 1–2. New York: Rinehart & Company, 1954.

Montgomery, Charles H. *The Spanish Redemption: Heritage, Power, and Loss on New Mexico's Upper Rio Grande.* Berkeley, Calif.: University of California Press, 2002.

Reid, Jan. *Rio Grande.* Austin, Tex.: University of Texas Press, 2004.

WEBSITES

American River Conservation
http://www.americanrivers.org/

Rio Grande information from an On-Line Encyclopedia
http://en.wikipedia.org/wiki/Rio_Grande

Environmental Protection Agency's (EPA) Site on American Heritage Designated Rivers
http://www.epa.gov/rivers/98rivers/riogrande.html

National Park Service Site
http://www.nps.gov/rivers/wsr-rio-grande-new-mexico.html

Rio Grande Restoration Project
http://www.riogranderestoration.org/

Handbook of Texas
http://www.tsha.utexas.edu/handbook/online/articles/view/RR/rnr5.html

Rio Grande Basin
http://www.utexas.edu/courses/h2o/encyclop.htm

Rio Grande Statistics
http://www.waterknowledge.colostate.edu/rio_gran.htm

TIM McNEESE is an Associate Professor of History at York College in York, Nebraska, where he is currently in his thirteenth year of instruction. Professor McNeese earned an Associate of Arts degree from York College, a Bachelor of Arts in history and political science from Harding University, and a Master of Arts in history from Southwest Missouri State University.

A prolific author of books for elementary, middle and high school, and college readers, McNeese has published more than 70 books and educational materials over the past 20 years, on everything from Indian mythology to the building of the Great Wall of China. His writing has earned him a citation in the library reference work, *Something about the Author*. His wife, Beverly, is an Assistant Professor of English at York College and the couple has two children, Noah and Summer. Readers are encouraged to contact Professor McNeese at tdmcneese@york.edu.